Contents

NATIONS OF THE WORLD

UNITED KINGDOM

Brian Innes

www.raintreepublishers.co.uk
Visit our website to find out more information about Raintree books.

To order:
☎ Phone 44 (0) 1865 888113
🖹 Send a fax to 44 (0) 1865 314091
🖥 Visit the Raintree bookshop at www.raintreepublishers.co.uk to browse our catalogue and order online.

First published in Great Britain by Raintree, Halley Court, Jordan Hill, Oxford, OX2 8EJ, part of Harcourt Education Ltd.
Raintree is a registered trademark of Harcourt Education Ltd.

Produced for Raintree by the Brown Reference Group plc
Project Editor: Peter Jones
Designer: Joan Curtis and Seth Grimbly
Cartographer: William Le Bihan
Picture Researcher: Liz Clachan
Indexer: Kay Ollerenshaw

Raintree Publishers
Editors: Isabel Thomas
Kate Buckingham

Printed and bound in Singapore.

ISBN 1 844 21471 0 (hardback)
07 06 05 04 03
10 9 8 7 6 5 4 3 2 1

ISBN 1 844 21485 0 (paperback)
07 06 05 04 03
10 9 8 7 6 5 4 3 2 1

British Library cataloguing in publication data
Innes, Brian
  UK. – (Nations of the world)
  1. Human geography – Great Britain – Juvenile literature
  2. Great Britain – Geography – Juvenile literature
  I.Title
  914.1

A full catalogue is available for this book from the British Library.

Acknowledgements
Front cover: Farmer carrying one of his sheep
Title page: The cliffs of Dover, Kent, England.

The acknowledgements on page 128 form part of this copyright page.

Foreword

Since ancient times, people have gathered together in communities where they could share and trade resources and strive to build a safe and happy environment. Gradually, as populations grew and societies became more complex, communities expanded to become nations – groups of people who felt sufficiently bound by a common heritage to work together for a shared future.

Land has usually played an important role in defining a nation. People have a natural affection for the landscape in which they grew up. They are proud of its natural beauties – the mountains, rivers and forests – and of the towns and cities that flourish there. People are proud, too, of their nation's history – the shared struggles and achievements that have shaped the way they live today.

Religion, culture, race and lifestyle, too, have sometimes played a role in fostering a nation's identity. Often, though, a nation includes people of different races, beliefs and customs. Many may have come from distant countries. Nations have rarely been fixed, unchanging things, either territorially or racially. Throughout history, borders have changed, often under the pressure of war, and people have migrated across the globe in search of a new life or because they are fleeing from oppression or disaster. The world's nations are still changing today: some nations are breaking up and new nations are forming.

The earliest monuments of the British Isles are the standing stones, erected from about 3000 BC. Britain was a distant outpost of the Roman empire and for over 500 years suffered repeated invasions. From the 16th century onwards, however, the country expanded overseas. Fuelled by its early industrialization, Britain created a massive empire on five continents that was to last into the 20th century. Since World War Two, the country has had to re-evaluate its position in the world, forming closer links with Europe and abandoning its imperialist stance. Today, Great Britain's wealth is based on thriving banking and energy sectors, along with new industries, such as media, fashion and biotechnology.

Introduction

UNITED
KINGDOM

The nation that many people refer to as 'the British Isles' or 'Britain' is properly known as the United Kingdom of Great Britain and Northern Ireland (UK). The UK is made up of the countries of England, Wales, Scotland and Northern Ireland. England, Scotland and Wales are all located on the island of Great Britain, which lies 32 kilometres (20 miles) north of France. Northern Ireland is geographically part of Ireland, an island to the west of Great Britain, separated from it by the Irish Sea. The word 'British' is used to refer to the people of the whole United Kingdom, including Northern Ireland.

The United Kingdom is one of the world's most indus-trialized nations, yet it is also a land of great natural beauty, from the craggy coasts of Northern Ireland and the highlands of Scotland to the soft, green rolling hills of England and Wales. The country has many Stone Age monuments, Roman ruins and medieval castles and cathedrals. Many of the country's buildings, however, and many of its cities were built during the 19th century, when Britain was the world's major **industrial** power and the centre of a large empire. Because of this history, the coun-try has many links with other nations, and the families of a significant minority of British people come from overseas.

Today, the UK is politically and economically closer to the other nations of Europe than ever before, and this trend looks like it will continue for the years ahead.

Christopher Wren's 17th-century dome of St Paul's Cathedral dominates the skyline of the City, London's historic financial district.

FACT FILE

• The UK has the 21st-largest population in the world, but is sixth in density.

• No point in the UK is further than 145 km (90 miles) from the coast.

• Zero degrees longitude passes through the Royal Observatory at Greenwich in east London.

• Nearly all the countries of the former British empire have now gained their political independence. However, most remain members of the Commonwealth of Nations, an association of countries that bears allegiance to the Queen.

The Union Jack is made up of the red cross on a white background of England, the white diagonal cross on a blue background of Scotland and the red diagonal cross of Ireland.

The front of all bank notes in the UK has the head of the Queen. There are two versions of the five-pound note – the one shown here features the inventor George Stephenson.

THE UNITED KINGDOM

The United Kingdom is a constitutional **monarchy**, which means that the head of state is Queen Elizabeth II. However, this role is ceremonial and the Queen has no real political power. The government is led by the prime minister, who is the leader of the political party with the most members of parliament (MPs).

The Union flag (above), popularly known as the Union Jack, symbolizes the administrative union of the countries of the United Kingdom. It is made up of the individual flags of three of the kingdom's four countries.

Currency

The British currency has gone through many changes over the centuries. The current decimal system was introduced in 1971 with 100 new pence (p) to the pound (£). There are coins for 1p, 2p, 5p, 10p, 20p, 50p, £1 and £2. There are also paper notes for £5, £10, £20 and £50. In Scotland and Wales, coins are minted that bear the respective national symbols of those countries, and these are accepted throughout the UK. Most notes are printed by the Bank of England, but separate notes are issued by several Scottish banks. The Channel Islands, which are located near the north coast of France, also issue their own currency.

Recently, there has been a major political debate in the United Kingdom as to whether the country should join the new European currency, the **euro**. The euro became the national currency of twelve **European Union** countries in 2002, replacing those countries' own national currencies. Entry into the euro looks increasingly probable, although it is opposed by many British people.

LANGUAGES AND PEOPLE

In terms of area, the UK is a small country, but it is densely populated with a total of almost 59 million people. It has roughly the same population as France but half the land area. England is the most densely populated country in the United Kingdom, with more than 386 people per square kilometre (1000 per square mile). Scotland, on the other hand, with an area half the size of England, has huge areas that are very thinly populated and the average density is only 66 people per square kilometre (170 per square mile).

Ethnic minorities make up about 3 million of the UK population. Of these, over 33 per cent are of Indian or Bangladeshi origin, 17 per cent from the Caribbean islands and 16 per cent from Pakistan. Other significant ethnic minority groups come from China and other Asian and African countries.

Because of its history, the UK has kept a remarkable variety of languages. The official language is English. In Wales, Welsh is taught in schools and spoken by many people, and official documents and road signs are in both English and Welsh. In Scotland, the English that is used (often known as 'Scots') has so many local words and usages that special dictionaries are published. In addition, the people of the Scottish Highlands and islands still use many words of **Gaelic** (a language related to Irish), and the

---

National anthem

The official national anthem is 'God Save the Queen [or King]'. It was arranged to a traditional tune by Thomas Arne (1710–78) in 1745 as a show of support for King George II. Of the five verses, usually only the first is sung:

God save our gracious Queen
Long live our noble Queen
God save the Queen.
Send her victorious
Happy and glorious
Long to reign over us
God save the Queen!

In recent years, the Scots have adopted a song called 'Flower of Scotland', written by a modern folk group, as their national anthem. It is played at international sports matches and other occasions. Similarly, the Welsh have for years used the song 'Land of My Fathers' as their national song. It may be sung in English or in Welsh.

Each country of the United Kingdom has its own symbol. In England, it is the rose, in Scotland, the thistle and in Wales, the leek. In Northern Ireland, a red hand is sometimes used.

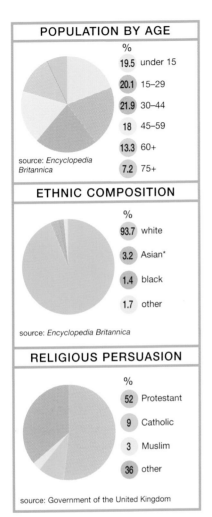

POPULATION BY AGE

%

19.5 under 15

20.1 15–29

21.9 30–44

18 45–59

13.3 60+

7.2 75+

source: *Encyclopedia Britannica*

ETHNIC COMPOSITION

%

93.7 white

3.2 Asian*

1.4 black

1.7 other

source: *Encyclopedia Britannica*

RELIGIOUS PERSUASION

%

52 Protestant

9 Catholic

3 Muslim

36 other

source: Government of the United Kingdom

* Refers to Asians from the Indian subcontinent.

revival of this language is being encouraged. On the Isle of Man, off the west coast of England, the ancient Manx language is still sometimes used. In the Channel Islands, a form of French is still common, and in Cornwall in the south-west of England, attempts are being made to revive Cornish. Every region of the UK has its own accent and dialect, with words that are unique to one locality.

In addition, every wave of immigrants has brought its own language. The Jewish community brought many Yiddish words (from *jüdische Deutsch*, meaning 'Jewish German'). Cantonese spoken by Chinese from Hong Kong and Singapore, Urdu from Pakistan, Hindi from India and Bengali from Bangladesh are all heard in British cities, although it is perhaps the languages of people from the Caribbean and Africa that are today having the most profound influence on British English.

Religion

The official religion of the UK is Anglican, a **Protestant** Christian religion governed by the Church of England. Other Anglican churches are established in Wales and Scotland. Scotland also has its own established church, the Church of Scotland, which is Presbyterian – that is, it is governed by a council of ministers and elders rather than by bishops.

The United Kingdom has one of the highest proportions of city dwellers in the world, a fact that reflects its history of heavy industry.

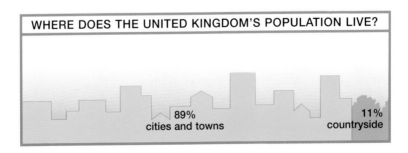

WHERE DOES THE UNITED KINGDOM'S POPULATION LIVE?

89% cities and towns

11% countryside

POPULATION DENSITY

The population of the UK is concentrated in the south-east of England and in the north-west around the industrial cities of Manchester, Liverpool, Leeds, Bradford and Sheffield. In addition, there are concentrations around Newcastle in the north of England, around the city of Birmingham in the centre and within an 80-kilometre (50-mile) radius of Edinburgh and Glasgow. The population of Wales is largely based in the south, previously the centre of its mining industry. The north of Scotland, the far north of England and the central area of Wales are very sparsely populated and have traditionally been given over to agriculture, largely sheep farming.

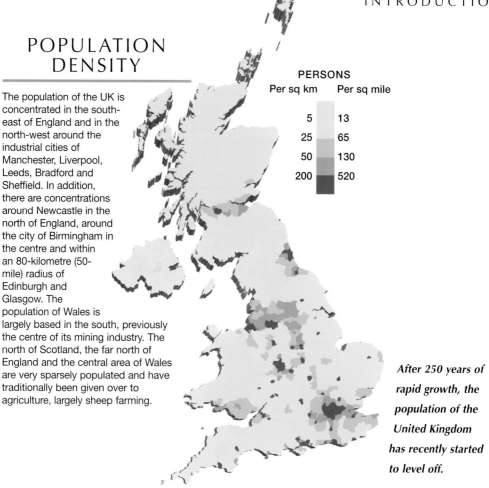

PERSONS

Per sq km	Per sq mile
5	13
25	65
50	130
200	520

After 250 years of rapid growth, the population of the United Kingdom has recently started to level off.

Following the establishment of the Church of England in 1527, **Roman Catholicism** was forbidden in Britain until 1829, although it was practised secretly. Around 9 per cent of the population are now Roman Catholics. Other important Christian churches include the Baptists, the Methodists and the Greek Orthodox. Recently, immigrant populations have also introduced other religions such as Islam and Hinduism. There has been a significant Jewish community in the United Kingdom for several centuries, and it now numbers about 300,000.

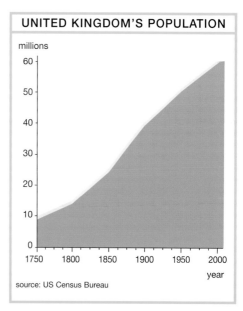

UNITED KINGDOM'S POPULATION

source: US Census Bureau

11

Land and cities

'This happy breed of men, this little world,
This precious stone set in a silver sea ...'

From John of Gaunt's Elegy for England in Shakespeare's *Richard II*

The people of the United Kingdom sometimes refer to their homeland as 'the British Isles'. And they have good reason: the UK is all islands – some 2000 altogether – from the one large island of Great Britain that makes up the British mainland (England, Wales and Scotland) to the many hundreds of smaller islands that are found mostly off the western coast.

Altogether, including islands, lakes and rivers, the UK covers an area of 244,690 square kilometres (94,475 square miles), and is slightly larger than Romania. England, at 130,323 square kilometres (50,318 square miles), is the largest of the countries that make up the UK.

The landscape ranges from sandy beaches and flat marshland to high **moorland** and green farmland. In urban areas, cities sprawl for kilometres into the sub-urbs. Although the country is densely populated in most parts, there are still regions of the United Kingdom that are quite remote and even some that are uninhabited.

The country is famous for its weather, which is extremely changeable. This is because it lies on the edge of the north European shelf, facing the Atlantic Ocean. The **Gulf Stream**, an ocean current, brings warm water up from the Equator, which means that the country is milder than other European countries lying on the same latitude, such as Germany. The Gulf Stream also brings rain, which gives the country its lush green countryside.

The area of Snowdonia in north Wales is characterized by mountains, moorland, glacial valleys, clear streams and dramatic waterfalls.

FACT FILE

● At its widest point, from Land's End in Cornwall to the Norfolk coast in the east, Great Britain measures 584 km (365 miles). The distance between England's southernmost point and the northern-most tip of mainland Scotland is 960 km (600 miles).

● The largest freshwater lake in the UK is Lough Neagh in Northern Ireland.

● The largest landowners in the UK are the **Crown** and the Church of England.

● The National Trust is a private organization that owns and runs many of the UK's parks and historic buildings.

13

THE FORMATION OF THE BRITISH ISLES

The land of the British Isles was formed millions of years ago. The rocks of north-west Scotland, for instance, are 3000 million years old. Other traces of the movement of landmasses from south to north – such as evidence of volcanic activity – can be found in Scotland. The hill known as Arthur's Seat, on the outskirts of Edinburgh, is the remains of an extinct volcano. At the Giant's Causeway near Portrush in Northern Ireland, dramatic hexagonal (six-sided) columns of rock emerge from the sea – they were formed from cooled lava. The extensive sands on the north-east coast of Northern Ireland are evidence that the land was once tropical desert. The big coalfields that lie under south-east Scotland, England's north-east and the Midlands and south Wales were formed from the remains of giant tropical ferns and trees.

Scotland was once joined to eastern Canada, and it was volcanic activity that eventually separated the two. Around the same time, what is now southern England was covered by a vast, shallow sea, in which many generations of shellfish lived and died. Their remains left a deep sludge at the bottom of the sea, which was gradually compressed. As the Earth's crust continued to move, the seabed was squeezed upwards, and the

The Giant's Causeway, a formation of rock columns rising out of the sea to a height of 150 metres (500 feet), lies on the northern coast of Northern Ireland.

~UNITED KINGDOM~

KEY

cities and towns
by population

◇ over 1,000,000
▣ 500,000 to 1,000,000
○ 100,000 to 500,000
● under 100,000

other symbols

▲ high points
-- country border

Shetland Islands

Fair Isle

Orkney Islands

Orkney Islands

● John o' Groats

Highlands

● Inverness
Loch Ness

SCOTLAND
Dee R.
● Aberdeen

Outer Hebrides

Inner Hebrides

Glen Mor

Fort William ● ▲
Ben Nevis

Grampian Mountains

○ Arbroath
● Dundee

Glasgow ●
EDINBURGH ▣
Firth of Forth

Jura
Islay

Hamilton ●
● East Kilbride

Kintyre
Arran

Southern Uplands

Atlantic
Ocean

North Sea

Giant's
Causeway

○ Londonderry

Newtownabbey ●
Lough Neagh
▣ BELFAST

NORTHERN
IRELAND

Enniskillen ●

Isle of
Man

Douglas ●

Newcastle ○
Sunderland ○

Carlisle ○

Tyne R.

Wear R.

Lake
District

Pennine Mountains

Irish Sea

Lancaster ●

Blackpool ●   Blackburn ○

● York

▣ Leeds

Bradford ▣

Kingston
upon Hull ▣
○ Grimsby

Liverpool ▣
Mersey R.   Manchester ◇

▣ Sheffield

Lincoln ○

Isle of
Anglesey

Trent R.

The
Wash

IRELAND

▲ Mt
Snowdon

Nottingham ▣

The
Fens

East Anglia

● Norwich

Stoke on
Trent ▣

▣ Derby

▣ Leicester

Aberystwyth ●

Cambrian Mountains

Birmingham ◇
● Coventry

Midlands

Cambridge ○
Ipswich ●

Stour R.

Cardigan ●

WALES

Severn R.

ENGLAND

○ Oxford
River Thames

Colchester ●

St George's Channel

Swansea ●
○ CARDIFF
▣ Bristol
● Bath

◇ LONDON

Canterbury ●

Dover ●

Bristol Channel

Exmoor

● Glastonbury

Brighton ○

● Hastings

Atlantic Ocean

Exeter ○

Dartmoor

Southampton ▣

Bournemouth ●

Isle of
Wight

○ Portsmouth

▣ Plymouth

Land's
End

English Channel

0	80	160	270 km

0	30	60	90	120	150	180 miles

Channel
Islands

FRANCE

THE TERRAIN OF THE UNITED KINGDOM

Mountains
Britain's mountains are found in the western half of the country, and in comparison to the rest of Europe are fairly low. The most spectacular of these are the Cairngorm Mountains in Scotland. Uplands in Northern Ireland are a continuation of Scotland's Southern Uplands.

Lowlands
The lowlands of Britain lie largely in southern England and around the coastal areas of the rest of the country. In central England and around the River Thames basin there are notable chalk outcrops. Along the English Channel coast are dramatic chalk cliffs that plunge directly into the sea.

Wetlands
The region encompassing the counties of Norfolk, Lincolnshire and Cambridgeshire is very low lying. Parts of this area are below sea level and pumps are used to keep the land free of water. Flooding has made the land very fertile, however, and the region is a centre for farming.

The white cliffs of Dover are the first part of Britain that the traveller sees from the English Channel. The cliffs lie 34 km (21 miles) across the Channel from France. During World War Two, the cliffs were the subject of a patriotic song.

sludge emerged as chalk, which now forms the cliffs of Dover, in southern England, as well as the downs (hills) that stretch westwards as far as Wiltshire. In parts of this area, prehistoric settlers carved figures into the ground – some of humans, some of animals – creating huge white forms in the green grassland.

At times during the Ice Ages, the ice that covered Britain and the whole of northern Europe was as much as 900 metres (3000 feet) thick. In warmer periods, huge glaciers gouged out valleys and lakes, forming the sea lochs (Scottish for 'lake') on the west coast of Scotland, and grinding great rocks into pebbles.

Some 2.5 million years ago, Great Britain was joined to Europe by a large, low-lying plain. As the ice melted, the sea level rose, flooding this plain to form the North Sea and cutting off Great Britain from mainland Europe. Beneath the North Sea lie reserves of oil and natural gas.

LOWLANDS AND HIGHLANDS

The geography of the British mainland can be divided into lowland and highland areas. Roughly, these two areas can be defined by drawing an imaginary line from the Tyne River in the north-east to the city of Exeter in the south-west (see map page 15). All the land to the south of this imaginary line is the lowland area, and all to the west and north – which includes Wales, Scotland and Northern Ireland – is the highland area.

The lowlands

There is a distinct difference in climate between the two regions. The lowland areas are warmer than the highlands throughout the year, although they may suffer severe frosts in the winter. The principal rivers flow through them, and humidity can be relatively high. The availability of water encouraged people to develop agriculture very early, and it was used for industrial transportation during the 18th and 19th centuries. Lowland areas include most of the highly populated parts of the country.

Parts of the lowland area are actually below sea level. Five centuries ago, there were 5180 square kilometres (2000 square miles) of wet marsh and open water in the north of East Anglia, between the cities of Cambridge

Buttermere Valley, one of the more remote areas in the Lake District in Cumbria, is seen here from the peak of Haystacks, looking down towards Crummock Water.

The geological structure of the British Isles is as complex as that of any major continent.

Lying to the east of Loch Linnhe in the Grampian Mountains, Ben Nevis is the highest peak in the United Kingdom.

and Lincoln. This area was known as the Fens. In the mid-17th century, a Dutch engineer called Vermuyden was brought in to drain the land. He cut channels through the marshes, built embankments along them and installed some 700 windmills to pump the water off the land. The windmills are long gone, replaced by mechanical pumps, but in places the fertile 'fenland' fields are 3 metres (10 feet) below the rivers that run through them.

The highlands

The highland areas of the UK are cooler than the land to the east. On the whole, they are much less densely populated, and there are fewer centres of industry. The hills and lower mountain slopes have provided suitable grazing for cows and sheep. For many centuries, wool was the basis of the UK's wealth.

No part of Britain rises to a very great height. The highest mountain in the United Kingdom is Ben Nevis in Scotland, which is 1344 metres (4409 feet) high. The second-highest peak, Mount Snowdon in Wales, is 1085 metres (3560 feet) high. The Pennine chain, which is often described as the 'backbone of England', reaches 890 metres (2930 feet) at its highest northern point. In the Lake District in north-west England, Scafell Pike is 977 metres (3210 feet) high. All of these areas have very dramatic scenery, are popular with walkers and attract large numbers of tourists. In Northern Ireland, the highest point is Slieve Donard, at 847 metres (2786 feet). With the exception of the Highlands of Scotland, even the most mountainous districts of Britain are easily accessible from the many roads that penetrate them.

The Pennine Way was the UK's first long-distance footpath, opened in 1965. The path runs along the crest of the Pennines and is periodically re-routed to keep one area from becoming eroded.

THE REGIONS

The division of the United Kingdom into distinct regions occurred early in the country's history and in some cases reflects ancient divisions – for example, most of Scotland was not conquered by the Romans, and, likewise, Wales remained a refuge of **Celtic** culture during the Roman period. Some of these divisions can still be heard in the different local accents and dialects and in names that are specific to certain localities.

ENGLAND

The country of England is the dominant region of the United Kingdom, both in terms of land area and population – 46 million people live in England. It is the centre of the government, industry, finance and the international relations of the United Kingdom. The main conurbations (urban areas) lie around London in the south-east, Birmingham in the Midlands, Manchester and Liverpool in the north-west and Newcastle in the north-east.

The suburban sprawl of housing at Elstree in Hertfordshire, north-west of London, is typical of the counties that surround the capital – kilometres of semi-detached houses set in their own gardens.

THE COUNTIES OF THE UNITED KINGDOM

The United Kingdom is split into several different types of county, depending on the region covered. Scotland is divided into council areas, or unitary authorities. Wales is split into 22 counties and county boroughs. Although the six counties of Ireland have no local government role, they are still recognized as geographical and traditional units. In England there are numerous definitions of counties; this map shows geographical and ceremonial counties.

SCOTTISH UNITARY AUTHORITIES
1 SHETLAND
2 ORKNEY
3 WESTERN ISLES
4 HIGHLAND
5 MORAY
6 ABERDEENSHIRE
7 CITY OF ABERDEEN
8 ANGUS
9 PERTH AND KINROSS
10 ARGYLL AND BUTE
11 STIRLING
12 CITY OF DUNDEE
13 FIFE
14 CLACKMANNANSHIRE
15 INVERCLYDE
16 WEST DUNBARTONSHIRE
17 EAST DUNBARTONSHIRE
18 FALKIRK
19 WEST LOTHIAN
20 CITY OF EDINBURGH
21 MIDLOTHIAN
22 NORTH LANARKSHIRE

23 CITY OF GLASGOW
24 RENFREWSHIRE
25 EAST RENFREWSHIRE
26 NORTH AYRSHIRE
27 SOUTH AYRSHIRE
28 EAST AYRSHIRE
29 SOUTH LANARKSHIRE
30 EAST LOTHIAN
31 THE SCOTTISH BORDERS
32 DUMFRIES AND GALLOWAY

GEOGRAPHICAL/ CEREMONIAL COUNTIES OF ENGLAND
33 NORTHUMBERLAND
34 CUMBRIA
35 DURHAM
36 LANCASHIRE
37 NORTH YORKSHIRE
38 EAST RIDING OF YORKSHIRE
39 CHESHIRE
40 DERBYSHIRE
41 NOTTINGHAMSHIRE
42 LINCOLNSHIRE
43 SHROPSHIRE
44 STAFFORDSHIRE
45 LEICESTERSHIRE
46 RUTLAND
47 CAMBRIDGESHIRE
48 NORFOLK
49 SUFFOLK
50 HEREFORDSHIRE
51 WORCESTERSHIRE
52 WARWICKSHIRE
53 NORTHAMPTONSHIRE
54 BEDFORDSHIRE
55 HERTFORDSHIRE
56 ESSEX
57 GLOUCESTERSHIRE
58 OXFORDSHIRE
59 BUCKINGHAMSHIRE
60 BRISTOL
61 WILTSHIRE
62 BERKSHIRE
63 SURREY
64 KENT

65 EAST SUSSEX
66 WEST SUSSEX
67 HAMPSHIRE
68 ISLE OF WIGHT
69 DORSET
70 SOMERSET
71 DEVON
72 CORNWALL
73 GREATER LONDON
74 MERSEYSIDE
75 GREATER MANCHESTER
76 WEST YORKSHIRE
77 SOUTH YORKSHIRE
78 TYNE AND WEAR
79 WEST MIDLANDS

WELSH COUNTIES AND COUNTY BOROUGHS
80 ISLE OF ANGLESEY
81 GWYNNEDD
82 CONWY
83 DENBIGHSHIRE
84 FLINTSHIRE
85 WREXHAM
86 POWYS
87 CEREDIGION
88 CARMARTHENSHIRE
89 PEMBROKESHIRE
90 SWANSEA
91 NEATH PORT TALBOT
92 RHONDDA, CYNON, TAFF
93 MERTHYR TYDFIL
94 BLAENAU GWENT
95 TORFAEN
96 CAERPHILLY
97 BRIDGEND
98 VALE OF GLAMORGAN
99 CARDIFF
100 NEWPORT
101 MONMOUTH

COUNTIES OF NORTHERN IRELAND
102 FERMANAGH
103 TYRONE
104 DERRY
105 ANTRIM
106 ARMAGH
107 DOWN

The Home Counties

The 'Home Counties' is the name given to the group of counties that ring London in south-east England: Bedfordshire, Buckinghamshire, Hertfordshire, Kent, East and West Sussex and Surrey.

There are many local industries, but an important proportion of the population of the Home Counties, and even beyond, commutes every day to work in central London. In the 1930s, a 'green belt' – an area in which further building of homes and factories is prohibited in order to contain the urban sprawl of cities – was established around London by law. However, many local authorities found ways to evade the law. In addition, the building of 'new towns' in the Home Counties during the 1950s – which were intended to relieve population pressure in London and the suburbs – has only increased the number of workers who commute to London every day. There are still agricultural areas – Kent, with its fruit orchards, is known as 'the garden of England' – but the Home Counties have become the most heavily populated region of the United Kingdom.

> During the late 19th and early 20th centuries, the county of Kent was famous for its farming lands, particularly its vineyards, orchards and hopfields. Workers from London would escape the smog to take working holidays in the fields, picking hops or fruit in early autumn.

East Anglia

The counties of Essex, Suffolk, Norfolk and Cambridgeshire make up East Anglia. The countryside is flat, with only a few hills. It is a predominantly agricultural area, although there are numerous local industries. A number of residents commute to work in central London. England's second-oldest university was established in the city of Cambridge in 1209 and has an international reputation for academic excellence.

The English

In *The English People* (1947), the English writer George Orwell, famous for his novels *Animal Farm* and *1984*, wrote: 'It is worth trying for a moment to put oneself in the position of a foreign observer ... Almost certainly he would find the salient [dominant] characteristics of the English common people to be artistic insensibility, gentleness, respect for legality, suspicion of foreigners, sentimentality about animals, hypocrisy, exaggerated class distinctions and an obsession with sport ...'

Glastonbury

The town of Glastonbury in Somerset has been a centre of British myth for hundreds of years. An early Christian legend even claims that the young Jesus once visited the spot. It is also the alleged burial place of King Arthur, an important figure in early English myth. A monastery was built here in the 4th or 5th century, the first Christian foundation in England, and three **Anglo-Saxon** kings were buried here. Today, the town is perhaps more famous as the site of the country's largest summer music festival.

In 1894, the chocolate manufacturing family the Cadburys established Bournville, the first suburb built specifically for industrial workers 6 kilometres (4 miles) south of Birmingham. The family fortune had been founded on the success of 'Cocoa Nibs', a chocolate drink created by the Quaker family in order to wean the working class away from beer.

The West Country

The West Country covers the counties of Dorset, Somerset, Devon, Cornwall, Wiltshire, Avon and Gloucestershire. Most of the West Country is agricultural. Although not mountainous, it is hilly and in places quite wild. Deer are common in rural areas, on Exmoor in Devon and Dartmoor on the boundary between Devon and Cornwall. Dorset and Devon have many tourist resorts and Devon includes the balmy English Riviera. The county of Cornwall is famous for its dramatic coastal scenery. It was one of the few remaining areas of Celtic culture after the Saxon invasions (see page 50), and for centuries was a centre for copper and tin mining. The largest city in the West Country is Bristol, a major port. Once a departure point for emigrants crossing the Atlantic, it is now a centre for the IT (information technology) industry.

The Midlands

Six counties – Worcestershire, Warwickshire, Staffordshire, Leicestershire, Nottinghamshire and Derbyshire – make up the heartland of England. Many of the country's coal seams lie beneath these counties and contributed to the early development of the **Industrial Revolution** in this region (see page 70). On the outskirts of this area lie the counties of Herefordshire, Shropshire, Lincolnshire, Northamptonshire and Oxfordshire.

Most of the region is flat, with the exception of the Malvern Hills in Shropshire to the west and the southern end of the Pennine chain of hills in Derbyshire to the north. The largest city in the Midlands is Birmingham, which became one of the country's principal manufacturing areas during the late 18th and early 19th centuries. It is still an important industrial and commercial centre. The nearby city of Coventry has a substantial vehicle industry. To the south-west is Stratford-upon-Avon, the birthplace of William Shakespeare (see page 102).

The outer counties are largely agricultural, although Oxford has a variety of smaller, high-tech industries, including computing and **biotechnology**. The city is the site of England's oldest university, founded before the 12th century, whose buildings include one of the world's great libraries, the Bodleian. The colleges of Oxford contain some of the most beautiful of English architecture.

The north-west

Lying to the west of the Pennine chain are the counties of Cheshire, Lancashire, Cumbria and Merseyside. Cheshire, with its rich agricultural land, has long been renowned as one of the wealthiest counties, but rural areas in the north soon give way to industry and commerce. The city of Liverpool, on the Mersey River, has been a leading port for much of its history. The building of the Manchester Ship Canal in 1894 linked inland Manchester to the sea. Manchester remains a major financial and industrial centre, second only to London in its economic importance. The northern county of Cumbria borders Scotland and contains England's highest mountains.

A major port since the 19th century, in the 1960s Liverpool became the centre of the Mersey scene with pop groups such as Gerry and the Pacemakers, Freddie and the Dreamers and the city's most famous sons, the Beatles.

Cumbria also contains the Lake District, with its mountains and spectacular lakeland scenery.

The north-east

Three counties make up the north-east of England: Yorkshire, Durham and Northumberland. For centuries, wool production from this region was one of England's most important trades. Clothing manufacture is still one of the principal industries in the region's southern cities. The coal that fuelled the Industrial Revolution (see page 70) was partly mined in this region, its coalfields rivalling those of the Midlands. Huge shipbuilding and engineering industries grew up around Newcastle-upon-Tyne. The upland areas of the north-east, which lie inland, are largely agricultural.

SCOTLAND

Scotland's two principal cities, Glasgow and Edinburgh, are both in the Lowlands, and historically they have always been the country's centres of business and culture. The larger of the two cities, Glasgow, was once a major industrial capital, but is now best known as a thriving

Built between 1883 and 1890, the Forth Bridge just west of Edinburgh is one of the marvels of Victorian engineering. It is so large that once it is painted, the process has to be started again.

cultural centre. Edinburgh (see page 39) is the financial capital of Scotland and the seat of its parliament. To the north of the Forth River, much of the land is agricultural, and there are small fishing ports.

The Scottish Highlands

The Grampian Mountains stretch from the west coast, not far north of Glasgow, to central Aberdeenshire in the east. To the north, the land is more bleak. Agriculture has remained important there, much of it barley for the many small whisky distilleries that dot the landscape, and the coastal ports still support an important fishing industry. The discovery of oil and natural gas beneath the North Sea has brought new wealth to the area.

Some 130 kilometres (80 miles) to the north-west of Aberdeen, the city of Inverness is known as the 'capital of the Highlands'. Inland a huge valley called Glen More runs south-westwards to Fort William on the west coast, splitting the Highlands in two. A canal was built in 1822 to link the inland lochs that line it. The largest of these is Loch Ness, at 32 kilometres (20 miles) long.

The west coast is deeply indented with lochs that open to the sea. In recent years, valuable fish farms have been established here. Inland the country is scarcely populated, and there are very few roads.

The Scottish islands

Hundreds of islands lie off the west coast of Scotland. Close to the west coast are the Inner Hebrides, the largest of which is Skye. Further to the west are the Outer Hebrides. The largest of these, Lewis, is divided into two. The smaller half is known as Harris and has given its name to the woollen tweed (woven fabric) that has been made in the islands for centuries.

There are two groups of islands north of the mainland Scottish coast. The Orkneys are close to the Scottish mainland, while the remote Shetland Islands lie 130 kilometres (80 miles) further north.

Loch Ness is famous for its monster, Nessie, a huge dinosaur-like creature that is said to lurk beneath its waters. Despite repeated sightings and alleged photographic evidence, the existence of the monster has never been proved.

Fair Isle – which has given its name to a type of patterned knitting – lies between the island groups of the Orkneys and the Shetland Islands in the sea north of the mainland Scottish coast.

WALES

Much of Wales is mountainous, with the exception of coastal areas, chiefly in the south and west. Its industrial development has resulted in the south-east becoming heavily populated. The coalfields of this relatively small region were once of the greatest importance, but many mines are now closed. Crowded towns and villages to accommodate the miners were built in the narrow valleys close to where the mines were dug. The seaport city of

The Rhondda Valley in south Wales has the typical development of Welsh mining towns – rows of terraced houses clinging to the side of the valley.

Cardiff is the capital of Wales, and its docks were once busy with the **export** of coal. Swansea, Wales's second city, lies 56 kilometres (35 miles) to the west.

Central and north Wales

The rest of Wales is quite thinly populated, and the Cambrian Mountains extend over much of its centre. Sheep farming is an important source of income, and slate, for roofs and floors, is still mined. There are a few small islands off the western coast, and one large one, Anglesey.

Northern Ireland

The counties of Northern Ireland largely cover the ancient kingdom of **Ulster**, and that name is still given to this region. The area is one-sixth of the total area of Ireland, but a third of the island's population live there. Much of the area is hilly. Most land is agricultural – largely for raising cattle, sheep and pigs. Belfast, the capital city, is a centre of industry. Shipbuilding and linen manufacture were long established, but recently have been replaced by other engineering industries, such as aircraft manufacture.

The Isle of Man

Although it is part of the United Kingdom, the Isle of Man, in the Irish Sea between England and Ireland, is a self-governing 'dependency'. It has its own Parliament and legal system and is not a member of the European Union (EU). Its economy is based principally on tourism, agriculture and fishing. The capital of the island is Douglas.

The Parliament of the Isle of Man, called the Tynwald, is arguably the world's oldest. It was established in AD 979 and has operated continuously ever since.

The Channel Islands

Like the Isle of Man, the Channel Islands – Jersey, Guernsey, Alderney, Sark and several much smaller islands – are a dependency of the United Kingdom. The four principal islands have their own assemblies and courts of law, and Jersey and Guernsey issue their own currency and stamps. The islands lie close to the northern French coast at Normandy. A form of French is still used there in official proceedings. The climate is milder than that of mainland Britain and is excellent for raising spring flowers and vegetables early in the season, and for cattle farming. The islands are also famous as a tax haven because of their low tax rates.

The Island of Sark

Unlike Jersey or Guernsey, Sark is a flat-topped outcrop of rock surrounded by steep cliffs. Strictly speaking, it is a 'fief' – an estate held by permission of the English Crown – and was granted that status by Queen Elizabeth I in 1565. The ancient laws dictate that no vehicles (apart from agricultural tractors) are permitted on the island. If police are needed, they must be sent for from Guernsey.

The national parks of England and Wales

The National Parks Authority was set up in 1949 and the first parks were designated in the 1950s. The authority protects the natural beauty of important landscapes and fosters employment for the local population. The preservation of these areas involves methods for the care and use of land that have developed over hundreds of years. With the exception of the New Forest and the waterways of the Norfolk Broads, the parks are located in the western uplands of Britain, and include a wide variety of terrains, from coastal areas to high mountains. There are plans to make Loch Lomond and the Trossachs in Scotland the next two national parks.

THE BRITISH CLIMATE

The British climate does not vary greatly between regions. This is due to the fact that the warm water of the Gulf Stream continually bathes the western coasts. As in San Francisco and the north-western states of the USA, where the warm Pacific Current runs close to the shore, this results in frequent mist and fog. At Inverewe on Scotland's north-west coast, the warmth of the Gulf Stream is strikingly evident. It is at about the same latitude as Copenhagen in Denmark, yet the climate is sufficiently warm for generations of skilled gardeners to have created a subtropical garden.

Western cities, such as Glasgow, experience more rain than those inland. Despite its northern situation, Scotland is still warmer than areas of Scandinavia that lie at the same latitude.

Generally, though, the UK is a damp and foggy country. Major weather systems move eastwards across the Atlantic, gathering moisture, and drop much of it upon the first land they meet. Heavy rainstorms are less frequent than a regular, penetrating drizzle – which is excellent for agriculture but unpleasant for the inhabitants. The humidity can make life miserable, especially in the cold of winter. Even if there is no rain, a heavily clouded sky is common. Over half of the days in the United Kingdom are overcast. Thick mists occur frequently throughout the country and on the coast even at the height of summer, but the famous British fog is far less common than is supposed.

There are exceptions to this picture of the British climate. Dry and cold air can flow southwards from the northern polar regions – sometimes bringing a 'cold snap', when the sun often shines from a clear sky but the air is chilly.

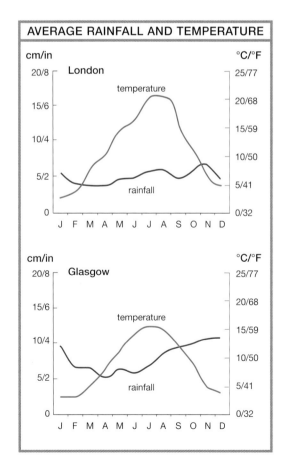

AVERAGE RAINFALL AND TEMPERATURE

Londoners make the most of the sun in the city's Regent's Park.

When cold air meets moist air, snow is likely in northern Great Britain – very occasionally even as late as June – but even in northern Scotland, deep falls of winter snow are unusual. Snow falls more heavily on the hills and mountains of north-western Great Britain, and in a cool summer, may stay on the higher tops.

Less frequently, hot, dry air may move northwards from the Sahara or even spread westwards from central Europe, raising midsummer temperatures in the UK into the 30s° C (90s° F). It is then that the British, while complaining of the heat and buying all the electric fans in the shops, act like they are in the tropics. Foreigners are surprised when the temperatures in southern Britain, with its reputation for rain, soar to levels more characteristic of the Mediterranean.

Flooding

Although the south-west of England and southern Wales have always suffered from periodic flooding, the problem has worsened since the 1990s. The UK's rainy climate makes swollen rivers a particular hazard. In the autumn and winter of 2000, this came to a head with thousands of homes in England being flooded and major towns such as York in northern England lying under several metres of water. Among other measures, the government has announced a large tree-planting campaign in the hope that tree roots will absorb the water, preventing run-off into rivers.

ANIMALS AND PLANTS

Fossil remains have shown that, at some time in Britain's ancient past, crocodiles, elephants and rhinoceroses roamed the land. Later, much of the British Isles was covered with dense forests, and wolves, bears and wild boar were common. These have disappeared in the past five hundred years.

Today, deer are among the most common species. Large landowners, particularly in the 18th and 19th centuries, liked to have a herd of deer to decorate their parks, and they introduced species from other countries, some of which later escaped into the wild. There are now five species of deer in Britain. The red deer is the largest, and the male has an impressive spread of antlers. It is most common in the Highlands of Scotland and on the moors of south-west England, but there is even a herd in Richmond Park, on the western outskirts of central London. Other native species are the roe and fallow deer. The tiny muntjac from China has spread widely in southern England, and the Chinese water deer, the only species without antlers, has established itself in East Anglia.

Foxes are very common and use railway tracks to find their way into towns and cities, where they scavenge food from dustbins. Numbers of two other mammals – the badger and the otter – declined sharply during the 20th century. Formerly they were hunted but they are now protected by law. Otters have suffered from the spread of mink, escaped from farms where they are bred for their fur. Native relations of the mink are the stoat, weasel, polecat and pine marten. Stoats and weasels are still common, but the polecat is restricted to Wales and the pine marten to Scotland and Northern Ireland.

Male red deer, or stags, shed part of their antlers each year. Males competing for females often lock antlers and fight over a mate.

Smaller species, such as voles, field mice and dormice, are also in decline and most are protected. The house mouse, however, remains plentiful, and there is concern about increasing populations of rats in British towns and cities. Rabbits were once very common. The deliberate introduction of the disease myxomatosis almost destroyed the population but it is now increasing again. Bats have greatly decreased in numbers. They favoured dilapidated barns and other ruined buildings, and since these have been cleared away, the bat population has declined. Bats are now legally protected, as are all species of reptiles and amphibians.

The common daffodil is grown all over the United Kingdom. In Wales, it is worn on St David's Day (1 March) as the national flower.

Conservation problems

The increasing use of insecticides and herbicides in agriculture has brought great changes to the appearance of the British countryside in the past fifty years. For example, the springtime air over the downs (hills) of southern England was once loud with skylarks, but their song is now seldom heard. Shooting of wild duck and geese and game birds is restricted to certain seasons, and all other species are fully protected by law. The protection of birds of prey has been especially successful, and the taking of eggs or young is strictly prohibited. The red kite is increasing in numbers in Wales, the golden eagle can be seen in Scotland and Northern Ireland and the nests of the osprey (or fish eagle) are fiercely guarded by volunteer enthusiasts.

The use of insecticides has resulted in a noticeable reduction in the number of butterflies and moths, and the wildflowers on which they feed are much rarer than before. Many species of wildflower and other plants are now protected by law – even picking them is illegal.

BRITISH CITIES

British cities are a mixture of ancient market towns that have grown up to be regional centres, such as Norwich and Exeter, and industrial centres such as Leeds and Nottingham, which largely came into being at the time of the Industrial Revolution (see page 70). The largest of the northern industrial cities is Manchester. Until the mid-18th century, Manchester was no more than a village, but during the 19th century, it grew to be one of the largest cities in the world and the site of an impressive array of Gothic buildings.

After industrial decline in the 1980s, the city has been reborn with a thriving IT industry, second only to that of the neighbouring city of Leeds. After London and Manchester, the third-largest city is Birmingham, with a population of more than 1 million. It was little more than a market town until the 19th century, when it became the commercial centre of the Midlands, a role it retains as the industrial hub of central England.

The city of Oxford was originally a centre for religious teaching, a fact reflected in its colleges built around open courtyards, which resemble the cloisters of medieval monasteries.

Greater London

Greater London, the capital of the UK, is Europe's largest city, with a population of about 7 million people. London covers more than 1550 square kilometres (600 square miles), and at its widest point extends for more than 50 kilometres (30 miles). As the centre of the British empire, it was the most important city in the world in the 19th century, and today it remains one of the world's major financial and cultural capitals. This role

33

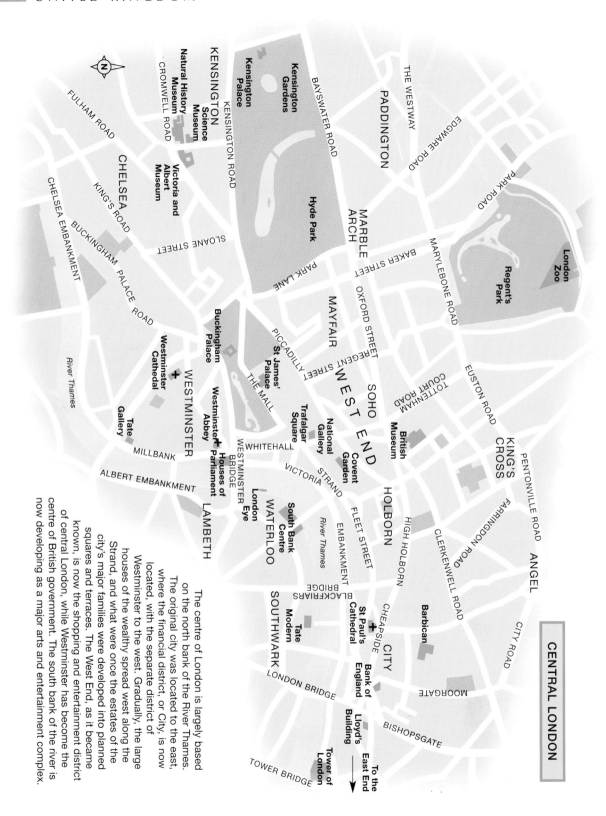

CENTRAL LONDON

The centre of London is largely based on the north bank of the River Thames. The original city was located to the east, where the financial district, or City, is now located, with the separate district of Westminster to the west. Gradually, the large houses of the wealthy spread west along the Strand, and what were once the estates of the city's major families were developed into planned squares and terraces. The West End, as it became known, is now the shopping and entertainment district of central London, while Westminster has become the centre of British government. The south bank of the river is now developing as a major arts and entertainment complex.

was amplified after reforms of the financial services industry in the mid-1980s (see page 91), which massively boosted the financial services economy. London has more than 40 major theatres, two opera houses of international standing, three great concert halls and three leading resident orchestras.

The tidal River Thames flows from west to east across the city, and most of central London's important buildings are located north of the Thames. Much of the city is made up of numerous former villages, each with its own distinct character, which have been joined up.

The tube

Practically all of north London and many parts of the south are linked by a vast underground railway system called the Underground or 'tube'. Eleven lines make up the network. The London tube is the oldest and largest underground railway system in the world. The first section was opened in 1863 between Bishops Road and Farringdon Street, with the Metropolitan and District Railway opening in 1868 between south Kensington and Westminster. Most of the Underground lines were built during the first decade of the 20th century. The last to be built was the Jubilee Line, opened in 1977 to commemorate 25 years of the reign of Queen Elizabeth II and extended in the late 1990s into south London. Although the tube is currently subsidized by public funds, there are government plans to encourage private investment.

In the foreground of this view of central London is the London Eye, a vast ferris wheel built to commemorate the Millennium. To the left is Westminster Bridge, beyond which stand the Houses of Parliament. Opposite the London Eye lies Whitehall, the area of government ministries.

The City

London is divided into 33 boroughs, or political units, of which two are known as 'cities' – the City of London and the City of Westminster. The City of London, the financial capital of the UK and one of the most important financial centres in the world, is the small area originally bounded by the ancient city walls. It is known as the 'Square Mile' and is occupied by banks and the offices of other financial organizations. About 5000 people live in the City but 300,000 commute to work there every day. St Paul's Cathedral is the most prominent landmark. At the eastern end of the City is the 12th-century Tower of London.

Westminster

The City of Westminster is larger in area and includes many of London's most expensive residential districts. Buckingham Palace, the official London residence of the Queen and the royal family, lies there, as do the Houses of Parliament – properly known as the Palace of Westminster. The area also includes most of the principal offices of the government, together with the official residence of the prime minister at 10 Downing Street. Westminster Abbey was first built in the first half of the 11th century but was completely redesigned over the next two centuries. Many famous writers and leaders are buried there. The principal cathedral of the **Roman Catholic** Church in the UK, Westminster Cathedral lies a short walk away. To the north

The high clocktower that stands at the northern end of the Houses of Parliament in London is known all over the world as 'Big Ben', although this is in fact the name of the great bell inside that tolls the hours.

Galleries and museums

Many of the finest art collections in the country are housed in London galleries. The principal galleries are the National and Tate. The former holds much of the nation's collection of international paintings, while the latter is dedicated to British and modern art. In 2000 the Tate opened a second London gallery in a renovated power station on the south bank of the Thames.

In the north of the West End is the British Museum. One of London's premier tourist attractions, it has an outstanding collection of ancient art and archaeology. To the west, in Kensington, are the Victoria and Albert Museum of decorative art and design and the Science and Natural History museums.

is Trafalgar Square, which was built to commemorate the naval victory against Napoleon. A statue of Admiral Horatio Nelson stands on a 50-metre-tall (164-foot) column in the centre of the square. The National Gallery lies along the north of the square.

The canals that flow through north London are part of a larger system that links with northern England. In west London, one picturesque section (above) is known as Little Venice.

The West End

To the west and north of Trafalgar Square is the West End, the main shopping and entertainment district. Most of London's major theatres are located here, as is the Royal Opera House. Oxford Street is the busiest shopping area and is lined with department stores. Soho and Covent Garden are lively areas with a huge variety of shops, restaurants, cafés and bars. Further west are residential areas broken up by areas of green parkland, such as Hyde Park, Kensington Gardens and Regent's Park.

The South Bank and East End

On the south bank of the Thames is the South Bank Centre, which houses the Royal Festival Hall (a concert hall), the National Theatre and the National Film Theatre. Also on the south bank is the towering form of the Tate Modern. This vast art gallery is reached from the City by the Millennium Bridge (a footbridge).

Multicultural London

Over the years, London has attracted immigrants from many different countries. Chinese immigrants formed a Chinatown in the East End in the late 19th century. East European Jews settled in the same area at the beginning of the 20th century. Today, Chinese people, mostly from Hong Kong, have created a Chinatown in Soho in the heart of the West End.

Since India's independence from Britain in 1947, large groups of people from the Indian subcontinent have arrived in the UK. They speak many different languages, such as Bengali and Hindi, and have brought with them different religions, such as Hinduism and Islam. People who belong to the Sikh religion are concentrated in Southall, near Heathrow Airport, and they have built the largest Asian shopping centre in London. People from Bangladesh moved to Spitalfields, an area just east of the City. Many are employed in the garment trade and restaurants. This area of London is popularly known as Banglatown.

Another large group of immigrants comes mostly from the Caribbean and also from some African countries. Jamaicans were the first to arrive in the 1940s, and they tended to settle in Brixton in south London, where there is still a large black population. People from Trinidad, Dominica and Saint Lucia usually settled in Notting Hill, which used to be a rundown area but is now one of London's most expensive and sought-after districts. Every August, the Notting Hill Carnival attracts more than 1 million visitors to listen to soul, reggae and other types of music, enjoy the street entertainment and sample the different types of foods sold from street stalls.

The East End, to the east of the City, was formerly the centre of London's docks and heavy industry. The area was heavily bombed during World War Two (1939–45), and until recently many areas were run down. However, rebuilding and redevelopment in the 1980s and 1990s has seen a revival of the area. Much of Docklands has been redeveloped into apartments and offices, and some businesses have moved there away from the crowded City.

Edinburgh

Though smaller than Glasgow with a population of less than 500,000, Edinburgh is Scotland's capital and the seat of its new parliament. It is the country's financial and cultural centre. There is great rivalry between the two cities, and Edinburgh fights hard to retain its cultural importance as Scotland's main arts venue.

Edinburgh's principal landmark is its castle, which rises on sheer cliffs above the city. King Malcolm III of Scotland first built a castle here in the 11th century. The castle houses the Chapel of St Margaret, which is the city's oldest structure. A road known as the Royal Mile connects the Castle Rock with the palace of Holyrood House. This 16th-century palace is the Queen's official Scottish residence. The Royal Mile is a magnet for tourists and is lined with bustling shops, cafés and bars. Many important and impressive buildings lie on or close to the Royal Mile, including St Giles' Cathedral, which dates from the late 14th century. South of the Royal Mile is Edinburgh University.

The oldest part of Edinburgh Castle dates from the 11th century. It was largely rebuilt in the 14th century, with additions to it in the last 100 years.

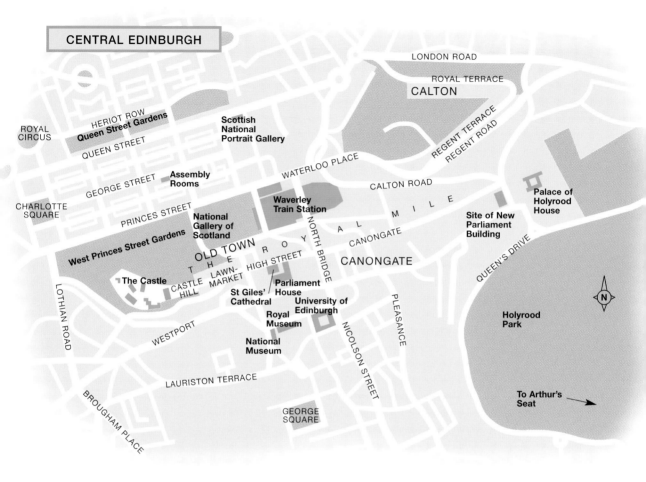

CENTRAL EDINBURGH

LONDON ROAD

ROYAL TERRACE

CALTON

REGENT TERRACE

REGENT ROAD

ROYAL CIRCUS

HERIOT ROW

Queen Street Gardens

QUEEN STREET

Scottish National Portrait Gallery

WATERLOO PLACE

CALTON ROAD

GEORGE STREET

Assembly Rooms

PRINCES STREET

CHARLOTTE SQUARE

West Princes Street Gardens

National Gallery of Scotland

Waverley Train Station

NORTH BRIDGE

THE ROYAL MILE

CANONGATE

Palace of Holyrood House

Site of New Parliament Building

QUEEN'S DRIVE

OLD TOWN

CANONGATE

The Castle

CASTLE HILL

LAWN-MARKET

HIGH STREET

St Giles' Cathedral

Parliament House

University of Edinburgh

Royal Museum

PLEASANCE

Holyrood Park

LOTHIAN ROAD

WESTPORT

National Museum

NICOLSON STREET

N

LAURISTON TERRACE

BROUGHAM PLACE

GEORGE SQUARE

To Arthur's Seat →

The Edinburgh International Festival is held every August. One of the greatest arts festivals in the world, it attracts visitors from all over the globe to enjoy the theatre, films, art exhibits and dance performances. The Edinburgh Fringe Festival is held at the same time, in which dozens of locations all over the city show fringe theatre (see box opposite), dance and comedy shows.

The city has plenty to occupy the visitor who is interested in art and history, such as the National Gallery of Scotland, the Scottish National Portrait Gallery and the Royal Scottish Museum, in addition to museums of modern art and history. The National Gallery of Scotland dates from 1859 and houses an impressive collection of European art dating from the 15th century.

Princes Street (left) is Edinburgh's main thoroughfare. In the foreground of the image is the National Gallery of Scotland and in the distance is St John's Church.

In July 1999, Scottish parliamentary elections were held for the first time in nearly 300 years. A new Parliament House is currently being built opposite Holyrood House.

Close to the Palace of Holyrood House is the magnificent Holyrood Park. Covering an area of 260 hectares (640 acres), its varied landscape includes Arthur's Seat, an extinct volcano that rises to 251 metres (823 feet). It is an easy climb to the top, from where there is a splendid view over the city below and across the Firth of Forth – the estuary on which Edinburgh lies. The park also has moorland and lochs (lakes).

The Edinburgh Festival

The Edinburgh Festival is held in August and early September and is famous as a centre for international dance, theatre and music. The festival was established in 1947 by the Austrian music director Rudolf Bing, who assembled musicians from central Europe after World War Two. The arrival of eight theatrical groups at the same time established the Fringe. This unofficial element in the festival traditionally includes many international theatre groups, student groups and even stand-up comedians. None of these acts is checked out by the organizers, so the Fringe is a breeding ground for experimentation, with some notable successes and many more questionable performances. Almost a thousand acts perform at the festival, using around 200 locations. The festival is now accompanied by the Edinburgh Film Festival.

Cardiff

Cardiff is the capital city of Wales and is located in south Wales on the Bristol Channel. A Roman outpost was established on the site of the city in about AD 75, and it was occupied by the Normans after their invasion of Britain in 1066 (see page 52). When the Glamorganshire Canal opened in 1794, Cardiff became an important port for transporting coal from the Welsh coalfields. Although the coal-mining industry has declined in recent years, Cardiff remains an important seaport and is also an industrial centre for the manufacturing of steel machinery and metal products, processed foods and textiles and paper. Having expanded through the 1990s, the population of the city now stands at about 300,000.

In the late 19th century, the Marquis of Bute, one of the richest men in the world at the time, spent a fortune on Cardiff Castle, adding, among other features, this clocktower, which bears his coat of arms.

The earliest remaining parts of Cardiff Castle, which is in the centre of the city, date from the 11th century, but much of what can be seen today dates from the 19th century. The rich coalfields that lie around the city were owned by local aristocrats, the Marquises of Bute and the local landowners, who insisted that coal exports be transported through the city's port, which the family had built and owned. Thus the city's docks thrived and Cardiff became the major city of south Wales.

Llandaff Cathedral, on the outskirts of the city, has seen much rebuilding and restoration over the centuries. It dates from the 12th century. Much of it was rebuilt in the 19th century, and there was extensive

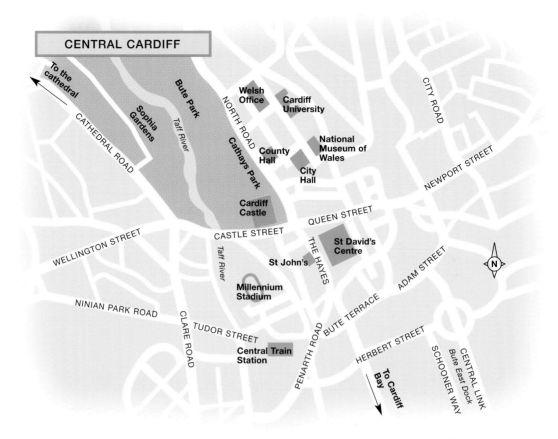

CENTRAL CARDIFF

restoration after it was bombed in World War Two (1939–45). Inside there is a magnificent central arch that houses the organ and a sculpture by Jacob Epstein (1880–1959; see page 99) called *Majestas*. The heads of the British monarchs (kings and queens) are carved on a wall outside on the south aisle.

From the early 1990s, Cardiff has reinvented itself as the fastest growing capital city in Europe. There is a huge freshwater marina on Cardiff Bay in the south of the city with an opera house. This pleasant area, which has recently undergone major redevelopment, is a good place in which to take a stroll on a sunny day. Buses run there from the city centre. In 1988, the University College, Cardiff – founded in 1883 – was merged with the University of Wales Institute of Science and Technology – founded in 1866 – to form the University of Wales College of Cardiff.

The capital of Wales since 1955, Cardiff expanded rapidly in the late 20th century. It has recently been further boosted by the building of the Welsh National Assembly in the Cardiff Bay area to the south of the city centre.

Belfast

Belfast is the capital city of Northern Ireland and a major port and industrial centre. The city emerged as an important trading town in the 17th century. Trade was greatly helped by the building of the Long Bridge over the Lagan River. The bridge was begun in 1682 and remained in use until the 1840s, when it was replaced by the Queen's Bridge. In the 19th century, industrial development, particularly in shipbuilding and linen, transformed the city from a small market town into a thriving industrial centre. By 1842, Belfast's population had risen to 70,000, twenty years later it stood at 120,000 and by the century's end it had reached 350,000.

When it officially became a city in 1888, Belfast was the largest commercial and industrial centre, the chief shipbuilding centre in Ireland (the *Titanic* was built in Belfast) and the third-largest port in the United Kingdom (after London and Liverpool). Prosperity brought many improvements and the opening of many public buildings, including the impressive City Hall in 1906. Musgrave Park was laid out in 1924. Ten years later, the museum and art gallery were opened and Belfast Castle

The grandiose City Hall, built to mark Belfast gaining city status, is the main landmark of the city's centre.

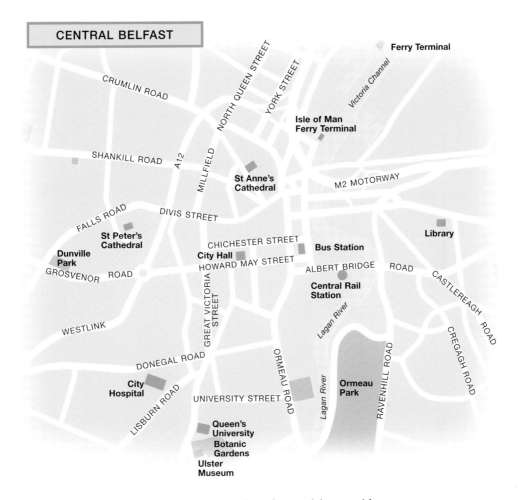

CENTRAL BELFAST

Map labels:
CRUMLIN ROAD · NORTH QUEEN STREET · YORK STREET · Victoria Channel · Ferry Terminal · Isle of Man Ferry Terminal · SHANKILL ROAD · A12 · MILLFIELD · St Anne's Cathedral · M2 MOTORWAY · FALLS ROAD · DIVIS STREET · Library · St Peter's Cathedral · CHICHESTER STREET · Bus Station · Dunville Park · City Hall · HOWARD MAY STREET · ALBERT BRIDGE · ROAD · CASTLEREAGH ROAD · GROSVENOR ROAD · Central Rail Station · CREGAGH ROAD · GREAT VICTORIA STREET · Lagan River · WESTLINK · DONEGAL ROAD · ORMEAU ROAD · Lagan River · Ormeau Park · RAVENHILL ROAD · City Hospital · LISBURN ROAD · UNIVERSITY STREET · Queen's University · Botanic Gardens · Ulster Museum

and its grounds accepted visits by the public. Belfast's population reached its peak during the 1950s, when it topped 450,000. During the period 1944 to 1968, the city council attempted to improve the long-time hostility between the Catholic and **Protestant** communities, building 11,600 houses in 30 development areas, mixing religious groups wherever possible. The outbreak of violence in the late 1960s and early 1970s (see page 78) halted much development, but building has begun again with the progress made in the peace process in the 1990s. Among the city's main attractions today are the massive Odyssey Millennium Centre, the Golden Mile of restaurants, entertainment venues and pubs and the lively nightclubs around Queen's University.

Originally built on the east bank of the Lagan River, Belfast spread to the west side of the river in the late 19th and early 20th centuries.

45

Past and present

'And the Britons completely isolated from the world ...'

Roman poet Virgil, *Eclogue* 1

Although there are no written records of early British history, the remains of Stone Age structures, such as Stonehenge, can be found all over the United Kingdom, and archaeologists have been able to discover something of what life must have been like in Stone Age Britain. From the time the Romans left Britain at the end of the 4th century AD, the history of the British Isles was one of invasion by different peoples until about the 11th century, when it was conquered by the Normans.

Thereafter, Britain became a relatively unified country. During the medieval period, there was great French influence on British life and raids into French territory. After about 1400, a recognizable form of English emerged, and, in the 150 years that followed, the making of a new national identity. From the late 16th century onwards, British maritime trade became increasingly important. After the civil war of the 17th century and constitutional reforms in the early 18th, Great Britain emerged as the world's leading **industrial** power, expanding its overseas territories throughout the 19th and 20th centuries into the largest land empire the world had ever known.

Two world wars virtually bankrupted the country, which lost its position as a world power and sought closer ties with Europe. Today, the United Kingdom is a leading European nation with a thriving economy and a unique position in the international community.

The first iron bridge in the world, built over the Severn River and opened in 1781, is one of the great monuments of the Industrial Revolution.

FACT FILE

• Great Britain was the first European nation to experience a revolution.

• Although it is often claimed that the UK has not been invaded since 1066, the Dutch prince William of Orange invaded southern England in the late 17th century, eventually becoming King William III.

• The first stationary steam engine was invented by Thomas Newcomen (1663–1729) in 1712 and erected at Dudley Castle in Warwickshire.

• More people were employed in agriculture than in industry in the UK until the middle of the 19th century.

Stonehenge

Stonehenge in Wiltshire is one of the great monuments of ancient Britain. Building began about 3000 BC, when an outer ditch and bank were dug. About 1000 years later, 60 stones, each of 4 tonnes (3.9 tons), were somehow brought from south Wales and placed in two concentric circles inside the bank. A further 80 blocks – each up to 50 tonnes (49 tons) and some nearly 9 m (30 ft) in height – were later erected in a continuous circle. Nobody knows how the stones were raised into position. Together with 56 equally spaced holes as markers, the stones could be used to predict accurately the movements of the Sun, Moon, planets and major stars, as well as forthcoming eclipses.

STONE AGE PEOPLES

Archaeological evidence suggests the first people arrived in the British Isles as ice retreated northwards at the end of the last Ice Age, 10,000 years ago. Gradually, more people arrived and brought their Stone Age culture with them. Some 5000 years ago, people from north-western Europe introduced the raising of livestock, agriculture and the making of pottery. They brought the custom of burying their dead in long or circular mounds, known as 'barrows'.

There are thousands of these barrows thoughout the British Isles, some merely of earth, others raised over a structure of stone slabs. The most impressive is Silbury Hill in Wiltshire, south-west England, which is the largest prehistoric mound in Europe. It seems certain that other structures were used as calendars. These are huge circles of stones – or sometimes of wood – that are often known as **henges**. They are found all over the country, and the most famous is Stonehenge in Wiltshire (see box).

THE BRONZE AND IRON AGE

After the Stone Age peoples, the next major wave of immigrants – some 4000 years ago – introduced the smelting of gold, copper and tin, which they found in western Great Britain and Ireland. From tin and copper they made bronze and traded it with mainland Europe. Around 500 BC, people experienced in smelting and working iron arrived. They introduced the first coinage: iron blanks of a standard weight, from which swords could be made. Soon the growth of trade with other countries led to the making of real coins, in gold, silver and bronze.

Some historians of Great Britain's stone circles have claimed that they are the sources of energy forces. There have even been experiments to prove that the stones give off electrical charges.

The Roman invasion

Between 58 and 50 BC, the Roman general Julius Caesar conquered the huge area of western Europe known as Gaul, up to what is now known as the English Channel. In 55 and 54 BC, he made two raids on southern England and claimed it for the Roman empire. The people of the islands, who called themselves 'Britons', were **Celts** related to the Bretons of Brittany in northern France.

In AD 43, the Roman emperor Claudius sent an army of 40,000 men with several elephants to conquer Britain. Within three or four years, the south of the country as far north as Yorkshire was in Roman hands. Wales took another 30 years to subdue. In AD 60, there was a brief revolt in the eastern part of Britain, led by Queen Boudicca of the Iceni tribe, but it was soon put down.

The Romans built roads throughout the country to make it easy to reach the forts they set up in strategic positions. In AD 79, the general Julius Agricola

From Julius Caesar's report on the Britons

'The island is densely populated, and everywhere houses meet the eye ... They have a conscientious scruple against eating either the hare, domestic fowl or goose, though all of these are kept for amusement or as pets ... All Britons dye their body with woad, a substance that contains a bluish pigment, and in battle greatly increases the wildness of their appearance. Their hair is worn very long and, with the exception of the head and upper lip, the entire body is shaved ...'

THE ROMAN CONQUEST

Antonine Wall

Hadrian's Wall

North Sea

Catterick
(Cataractonium)

Irish Sea

York
(Eboracum)

Chester
(Deva)

Lincoln
(Lindum)

Leicester
(Ratae
Coritanorum)

Gloucester
(Glevum)

St Albans
(Verulamium)

Colchester
(Camulodonum)

Cirencester
(Corinium)

Oxford

LONDON
(LONDINIUM)

Canterbury
(Durovenum)

Hinton
St Mary

Chichester
(Noviomagus
Regnensium)

Exeter
(Isca)

English Channel

invaded Scotland but his troops had to be withdrawn to deal with trouble nearer Rome. Then in AD 122, the emperor Hadrian brought a force to Britain and built a stone wall across the country close to the present border between England and Scotland. For the next 300 years, the wall marked the northern limit of the Roman empire. Much of the wall and the forts that were built along it still remain.

South of Hadrian's Wall, the population became increasingly Romanized. The central government was run mostly by Britons who had adopted the Roman way of life, and towards the end of the 4th century, Roman troops were withdrawn from Britain.

The map above shows important Roman towns and roads.

ANGLES, SAXONS AND JUTES

From the time the Romans left, for 600 years the history of the British Isles is one of invasion. The first invaders were Angles, Saxons and Jutes from present-day northern Germany and Denmark. These peoples occupied most of eastern and southern Britain, driving the original Celtic inhabitants westwards and northwards into the furthest parts of the land. The country became divided into separate kingdoms, some of which resisted the invasion, while others accepted it.

In 596 Pope Gregory I sent Augustine (later St Augustine of Canterbury) to convert Kent in south-eastern England to Christianity.

The English kingdom

Gradually, the whole country now known as England was brought under **Anglo-Saxon** domination. Then came another threat. Vikings from Norway (Norsemen) and from Denmark (Danes) began to raid the country,

Early Scottish history

The earliest inhabitants of Scotland were known to the Romans as Picts. This means 'painted people' because, like the Britons, they decorated their bodies with woad, a type of dye, or, perhaps, even practised tattooing. Very little is known about them. They have left no written language, although there are remains of intricately carved stone monuments featuring human figures and symbolic patterns.

About AD 300, the Picts began to join forces with **Gaelic**-speaking pirates from Ireland – known to the Romans as Scots – and make raids into Roman-held Britain. Gradually, the Irish people moved into the south-west part of Scotland and established a kingdom named Dalriada. Some time around the middle of the 9th century, the Dalriadan king, Kenneth MacAlpin, married a Pict princess and so became the ruler of the whole of what came to be called Scotland.

At about the same time, Vikings from Scandinavia began to raid the western coasts. They occupied all the islands – the Shetlands, the Orkneys and the Hebrides – and for a time dominated most of Ireland. However, the kings of Scotland were able to resist them. Then, in 1040, the last of the MacAlpin family, 'gentle Duncan', was slain by the Lord of Moray, Macbeth.

Dunnotar Castle is a 9th-century fortress south of Aberdeen, which was built to protect the coast against Viking raids. More recently, it was used as the setting for Franco Zeffirelli's film Hamlet.

and the Danes mounted a major invasion. It was not until 878 that the English king, Alfred, defeated the Danish army in the south and established peace with them. In 886, he recaptured London, and the Danes were allowed to settle in East Anglia – the present counties of Essex, Suffolk, Norfolk and Cambridgeshire.

VIKING INVASIONS IN ANGLO-SAXON BRITAIN

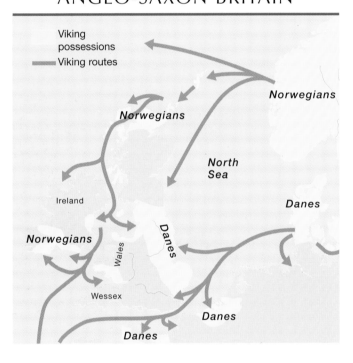

The Vikings were the seafaring peoples of Scandinavia. The Danes controlled north-eastern Britain and portions of the north French coast, while the Norwegians raided northern Scotland and parts of Ireland and Wales.

The battle for the Crown

Meanwhile, in the northern parts of the country, the Danes and the Vikings continued to hold large areas. The Vikings also settled in northern France, in the area now known as Normandy. From 1042 to 1066, the English king was Edward, known as 'the Confessor', and he had to decide who was to inherit his kingdom. The Viking leader Harald Hadraade had a strong claim, but Edward decided upon William, the Duke of Normandy. On his deathbed, however, Edward granted the kingdom to the son of the Earl of Wessex, Harold.

In September 1066, Harald Hadraade invaded northern England. Harold defeated him, but in the meantime William of Normandy had landed on the southern coast. Harold marched his army south as fast as he could, but on 14 October, near the town of Hastings, he was killed in battle. The Norman forces took over the country, and William was crowned King William I.

THE NORMAN STATE

The arrival of the Normans brought, at last, a degree of stability to England. The Normans were first-class soldiers, and their reputation prevented any further invasions. William appointed his own followers as military commanders (**barons**). They were given huge tracts of land throughout the country and had to raise a sufficient number of mounted men (knights) if ever the king required them. These barons built their own castles, which replaced the earlier Roman forts, and William had his own castle, the Tower of London (right).

William restricted the influence of the pope in Rome over the English Church. He recognized the authority of the pope's representative, the Archbishop of Canterbury, in matters of church law, but insisted on his right to appoint the higher officers of the church.

The long-lasting quarrel with France was over land claimed by the English. When William's great-grandson was

The Domesday Book

One of William I's first measures was a survey of nearly all the lands in his new kingdom. He sent out commissioners to find out who held each piece of land, its area, how much could be ploughed, the mills and fishponds, the number of peasants and how much it was worth. The written record was called the Domesday Book (pronounced 'Doomsday') because the English thought that it would last until the Day of Judgement (or Doomsday). The document was so useful that it was even used by later administrations as a basis for taxation.

A former royal residence, the Tower of London (in the background) has been the scene of some of London's most macabre and bloody scenes of torture and imprisonment.

The legend of Robin Hood is set at the time when Richard I was fighting overseas, and Richard's brother John had taken over the kingdom. When Richard returned to England, he disguised himself and rode into Sherwood Forest, where he was recognized as the true king by Robin. Richard forgave Robin his crimes and gave him a place at the royal court.

crowned King Henry II in 1154, he was already Duke of Normandy and Aquitaine and Count of Anjou, all parts of France. In this way, he became the ruler not only of England but also of nearly half of what is present-day France. He also claimed Wales, Scotland and Ireland.

Henry's son Richard – 'the Lionheart' – was king for ten years (1189–99), but he was heavily involved in the Crusades, an attempt to reclaim Jerusalem from Muslim forces. Richard spent only a few months in England and was succeeded in 1199 by his brother John. John's reign was not a successful one. He lost the support of many of his barons and was forced to give up Normandy. This quarrel with the barons led in June 1215 to one of the most important events in early English history. At Runnymede on the Thames not far from London, John was forced to cede power to the barons by signing the 'Great Charter', or Magna Carta (see box below).

John died a little over a year after signing the Magna Carta, leaving a nine-year-old boy as his heir. At that time, London – which was then effectively almost a separate city-state – and much of eastern England were in the possession of rebellious barons, who were

The Magna Carta

The Magna Carta has been hailed as the document on which the idea of English freedom was based, but it was dictated by the barons and was first of all in their interest. They were angry at King John's failure to protect their possessions in France, the source of much of their income. The king had also imposed high taxes, overruled the local law courts and gathered all legal fines for himself – money that had previously also gone to the barons.

The purpose of the Magna Carta was, therefore, to restrict the powers of the king, particularly in matters of arrest and imprisonment. The freedom of the church was confirmed, and the barons regained the fines imposed on offenders by the courts. Later in English history, the Magna Carta was held up as a statement of fundamental civil rights. Of the four original copies that still exist, two are in the British Library, one is in Salisbury Cathedral and one is in Lincoln Cathedral.

supported by the French. But the pope approved the boy as King Henry III, and peace was signed. It was during Henry's reign that the first use of the word 'parliament' – a French word meaning 'a conference of important people from all over the country' – occurred in official accounts.

Henry died in 1272, after 56 years as king, and was succeeded by his son Edward. Edward I kept power very much in his own hands, but regularly summoned parliaments to discuss changes in the law. He conquered northern Wales, and in 1301 named his eldest son the prince of Wales.

The title of 'Prince of Wales' is traditionally given to the monarch's male heir and therefore heir to the throne. Since the 16th century, the title of 'Duke of York' has been conferred on the monarch's second-eldest son.

THE HUNDRED YEARS' WAR (1337–1453)

Perhaps the most significant event of the next century was the outbreak of 'Black Death' – bubonic plague – in 1348. At least one-third of the population died within a few months. A shortage of workers led to a period of disturbances such as the Peasants' Revolt of 1381. Other

THE HUNDRED YEARS' WAR

The English enjoyed early successes in the Hundred Years' War, but in the late 1420s, the French rallied under Joan of Arc and by the 1450s had expelled the English from all but Calais.

55

English incursions in Scotland

For nearly two centuries after the death of King Duncan, Scotland enjoyed a period of calm – known as 'the age of ale and bread'. However, in the winter of 1286–7, the death of the king, Alexander III, provoked a crisis. His young granddaughter, the Norwegian princess Margaret, was his heir, and in 1290, the Scots agreed that she should eventually marry the English king Edward I's son, the future Prince of Wales. But Margaret died during the voyage from Norway, and Edward announced that this made him the overlord of Scotland.

Edward accepted John Balliol, a great-great-great-grandson of the Scottish king David I, as ruler of Scotland, but many Scots refused to accept the English domination and made an agreement with France. In 1297, William Wallace, the son of a minor landowner, who had raised first an outlaw band and then an army, defeated the English forces in a battle at Stirling Bridge. However, his success was short-lived. Edward made peace with France, and his army

occupied Scotland. When Wallace returned from France in 1303, he was betrayed and was brutally executed in London in 1305.

It was then that Robert Bruce, another descendant of David I, claimed the throne of Scotland. Edward I died in 1307, and was succeeded by his son, Edward II. In 1314, at the Battle of Bannockburn, a small Scottish army led by Bruce defeated a much larger English force. Fourteen years of conflict followed. In 1327, the English Parliament deposed Edward II and made his son King Edward III. A year later, peace was signed between Scotland and England.

However, when Robert Bruce, King Robert I (left), died, Edward III supported the claim to the throne of John Balliol's son, and English raids into Scotland continued for another 50 years. Then Robert Stewart, a grandson of Robert Bruce, was proclaimed King Robert II in 1371, the English occupying forces were driven out in 1384 and the Stuart dynasty (family of rulers) was effectively established for the next two centuries.

countries in Europe were similarly affected. At the same time, England was at war with France, a conflict that was to last, on and off, for 100 years. Central to the dispute was the English claim to the lands of south-west France.

Edward III died in 1377, and was succeeded by his grandson Richard II, who was just ten years old. He had to rely upon the advice of his uncle, John of Gaunt. When John died in 1399, Richard II was forced to **abdicate** and name Henry Bolingbroke, John's heir, as King Henry IV.

Henry IV's reign was as disturbed as those that had preceded it. When he died in 1413, his son became Henry V. Henry proved to be a first-class military leader and a strong political ruler. His most famous victory was the defeat of the French at Agincourt in 1415. Five years later, he married Catherine, daughter of the French king, and was recognized as heir to the French throne. On his death only two years later, two regents ruled the country in place of his son Henry VI. They were defeated by the French, led by the patriotic leader Joan of Arc. By 1454, only the Channel port of Calais still lay in English hands.

The areas under the control of the two factions during the Wars of the Roses were largely centred around castles and other fortified structures into which both the aristocracy and peasantry could retreat at times of attack.

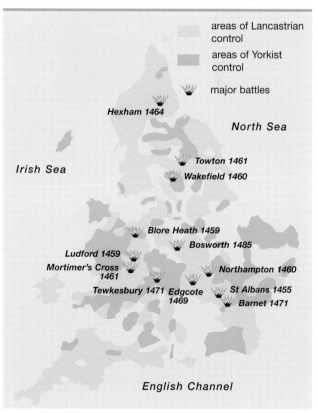

WARS OF THE ROSES

areas of Lancastrian control

areas of Yorkist control

major battles

Hexham 1464

North Sea

Irish Sea

Towton 1461
Wakefield 1460

Blore Heath 1459
Bosworth 1485
Ludford 1459
Mortimer's Cross 1461
Northampton 1460
Tewkesbury 1471 Edgcote 1469
St Albans 1455
Barnet 1471

English Channel

WARS OF THE ROSES

Henry VI was mentally unstable and took little part in politics. Until 1450, the running of the country was in the hands of the Duke of Suffolk, who belonged to the house (dynasty) of Lancaster. His great rivals were the dukes of Gloucester and York.

A blackened name

During the 16th century, Tudor historians blackened Richard III's character so successfully that it is impossible to be sure what sort of a man he was. Certainly, he arranged for Edward V and his nine-year-old brother to be imprisoned in the Tower of London, and there is no doubt that they were brutally murdered there some weeks later. In his play *Richard III*, Shakespeare portrayed Richard as a bitter hunchback. But the playwright would hardly have wanted to upset his Queen, Elizabeth, the granddaughter of Henry VII, who had been Richard's opponent on Bosworth Field.

In 1497, the Venetian Giovanni Caboto (also known as John Cabot) funded by Henry VIII sailed from Bristol in search of a route to Asia. He landed at Labrador, Canada, which had last been visited by Vikings in the 11th century.

Gloucester died in 1447, and Suffolk was murdered in 1450, leaving Richard, Duke of York, as a claimant to the English throne. Henry's wife, Margaret, supported the house of Lancaster, which had a red rose as its emblem. The house of York had a white rose for its emblem, and the conflict that followed is known as the Wars of the Roses. Richard was killed in battle, but his son Edward took London in 1461 and was pronounced King Edward IV. In 1465, Henry was captured and imprisoned in the Tower of London. Edward died in 1483, and his twelve-year-old son, Edward, was placed under the protection of his uncle Richard, Duke of Gloucester, who, on the death of the young Edward V, became Richard III.

THE TUDORS

Richard reigned for only two years before he was killed in the Battle of Bosworth Field in 1485 against an army raised by Henry Tudor, a nephew of Henry VI. Henry, who became Henry VII, came from a Welsh family and so was able to unite England and Wales. He also married Elizabeth of York, uniting the factions of Lancaster and York. Growth in the textile trade brought new wealth to Britain and the rise of a new merchant class, particularly in London. Henry VII improved the finances of his kingdom, introducing bookkeeping and appointing officials to collect revenues. Henry forced the Irish to accept the authority of the English Parliament, made peace with Scotland by marrying his daughter Margaret to the Scottish king, James IV, and established a loose alliance with France and Spain, marrying his son Arthur to the daughter of the powerful king and queen of Spain. Arthur died before his father, and his widow, Catherine, remarried Arthur's younger brother Henry, who in 1509 became Henry VIII.

King Henry VIII

Henry had had to get the pope's permission to marry Catherine. When the marriage failed to produce a male heir, he asked for it to be declared illegal. He had fallen in love with Anne Boleyn, a young woman from a powerful aristocratic family. The pope refused. The king then bullied the English clergy into accepting him as the head of the church in England. Henry's marriage to Anne produced a daughter, Elizabeth. Within three years, Anne was charged with adultery and beheaded. The king married Jane Seymour, who at last gave him an heir, Edward, but she died in childbirth.

Henry was the first monarch of the English Renaissance, a clever, athletic man, who – his rule underpinned by vast tax revenues from the wool trade and the sale of church lands – greatly expanded the power of the monarchy.

The break with Rome

Concerned about the power of the church and its extensive lands, Henry and the chancellor, Thomas Cromwell, set about closing all the monasteries, taking possession of their lands and valuables and selling what they could. Henry's actions outraged many in the church and caused a split between those loyal to the Catholic Church in Rome and others who welcomed the new **Protestant** religion, which originated in Germany. The final break with the church in Rome came when an official translation of the Bible into English was based on a Protestant version. Protestants wanted to reform the **Roman Catholic** Church. They did not accept the pope as head of the church. To strengthen relations with German Protestants, Cromwell persuaded Henry to marry Anne of Cleves. The marriage was a failure, however, and Cromwell was beheaded. The king married twice more before his death in 1547.

The reigns of Henry's two successors were notable for religious strife between Protestants and Catholics. First his young son Edward and his advisers set about firmly establishing Protestantism, stripping churches of their Catholic imagery. Then, on Edward's early death in 1553, Henry VIII's elder daughter, Mary, a Catholic, was proclaimed queen. In 1554, she married her cousin, Prince Philip of Spain, who therefore became king of England. Mary's five-year reign was marked by her campaign against Protestants – nearly 300 were burnt at the stake – which earned her the name of 'bloody Mary'.

Queen Elizabeth I

On Mary's death in 1558, she was succeeded by her half-sister, Elizabeth. She ruled for 45 years, during which

time she restored Protestantism, set up a strong council of ministers and encouraged important voyages of exploration, together with trading throughout Europe, in Russia and in Africa. During her reign, Francis Drake made a voyage around the world, from 1577 to 1580, and in 1585, Walter Raleigh established the first colony in North America, at Roanoke in Virginia.

In the same year, Elizabeth gave Drake permission to attack Spanish ships and possessions in the Caribbean Sea. She also sent an army of 6000 men to aid the Dutch in their struggle against Spain in the Netherlands. This provoked the Spanish king, Philip, into assembling a large fleet

ENGLISH EXPLORATION 1550–1650

Atlantic Ocean

EUROPE

NORTH AMERICA

Pacific Ocean

Willoughby and Chancellor 1553
Raleigh 1584
Hudson 1609
Hudson 1610
Baffin and Bylot 1616

(armada) to attack and invade England. The English fleet, one of whose commanders was Drake, managed to put the Spaniards to flight off Calais. They fled northwards around the British Isles, where storms drove many Spanish ships onto the Scottish and Irish coasts. Less than half struggled back to Spain.

While the Spanish and Portuguese explored South America, the English explored the northern continent.

ENGLAND AND SCOTLAND UNITED

Elizabeth died in 1603. She had not married, and there was no son to succeed her. Through her aunt Margaret, however, she was directly related to the Stuart king James VI of Scotland. The time was ripe for the union of the two kingdoms, and so James VI was proclaimed James I of England. He was not a popular king. He is best remembered for the translation of the Bible that

The gunpowder plot

Two years after James became king of England, a group of Catholics plotted to blow up the king at the opening of Parliament. The date was set for 5 November 1605. The plan was made by Robert Catesby, and among the conspirators was a soldier brought over from the Netherlands named Guy (or Guido) Fawkes. The men were betrayed and a search of the Parliament cellars found Fawkes and the gunpowder. Catesby and three others were killed while resisting arrest, and the rest were tortured and executed. Guy Fawkes' Day is still celebrated every year in England with fireworks, bonfires and the burning of stuffed dummies known as 'guys'.

James I wrote
a number of
essays during his
lifetime, among
them one
condemning
witchcraft and
another against
the new craze for
tobacco, recently
imported from
North America.

he authorized. It was published in 1611 and, even after four centuries, remains an outstanding piece of English literature. Nevertheless, during James's reign, in 1608 a permanent colony was established in Virginia, the first in North America, and the French were prevented from colonizing Maryland and Nova Scotia in Canada.

James died in 1625 and was succeeded by his son, Charles. In 1628, Charles quarrelled with Parliament, and for eleven years, he ruled without it being assembled. However, the nation's finances continued to be the great problem, and when there was a rebellion in Scotland, Charles had no money to raise an army. He was forced to recall Parliament, which sat for nine months, demanded the dismissal of most of Charles's closest advisers and required that the regular sitting of Parliament be part of the law.

CIVIL WAR

Under Henry VIII, the Church of England had broken with Rome, but it had kept many of the ceremonies of Catholicism. A movement gradually developed that wanted to do away with all of this. It was called Puritanism, and by 1640, there were many **Puritans** in Parliament. They were concerned about the influence of Queen Henrietta Maria, who was a Roman Catholic, on Charles I, and they also wanted to take the power to raise an army out of the king's control. In August 1642, the situation finally got out of hand. Civil war broke out between the king's supporters (the **Royalists** or Cavaliers) on one side and Parliamentarians on the other.

New Model Army

In the early stages of the Civil War, the Royalists enjoyed superiority because of the strength of their cavalry. After negotiations with the king failed, Parliament responded by creating the New Model Army under the command of Oliver Cromwell and Sir Thomas Fairfax. The new force combined the remnants of three other armies, which were then trained and disciplined under their new leaders.
A major difference in the new fighting force was the payment of wages and the professionalism of its fighters.

For over a year, the Royalists had the advantage thanks to their cavalry. Then a landowner from East Anglia named Oliver Cromwell began to build up a force of mounted soldiers, and in 1644, he and Sir Thomas Fairfax organized a 'New Model Army' (see box opposite), which finally defeated the Royalists. Charles I was imprisoned, put on trial and beheaded on 30 January 1649. Parliament declared that England was now no longer a kingdom but a commonwealth.

The army was now in control of the country and insisted upon a strict Puritan rule, suppressing all popular amusements, such as theatres. As the most important military leader, Cromwell was appointed Protector of the Commonwealth. However, Puritan rule created a great deal of unrest. For a time, the Scots supported Charles's exiled son, who declared himself King Charles II, and in Ireland Cromwell put down the Catholics with great brutality. Parliament was dissolved by Cromwell in 1655, but in the following year, war with Spain made it necessary for a new Parliament to be assembled. If Cromwell had lived longer, England might well have become a republic. However, he died in 1658,

The execution of Charles I in early 1649 took place outside his own palace in London's Whitehall, now the main street of government ministries.

The London Plague of 1665 and the Great Fire of London the following year were interpreted by Puritans as God's judgement on a sinful city. London was reconstructed as a more sanitized city built of stone rather than the wood used before.

and his son, Richard, who succeeded him as Protector, was unable to control either Parliament or the army. In May 1660, Charles II was welcomed back.

The kingdom restored

Charles was known as the 'merry monarch' because he reopened theatres closed by the Puritans and restored popular amusements. His reign was also characterized by the rise of science and arts. In 1660, the Royal Society was founded to further the study of science. It counted Isaac Newton (1642–1727) among its first members.

When Charles died in 1685, his Catholic brother, James, succeeded him. James II ruled for only three years, during which time he raised many Catholics to important positions. As a result, a number of eminent Englishmen invited the Dutch prince William of Orange, a Protestant who was married to James's Protestant daughter, Mary, to invade England and take the throne. William III and Mary II were made joint sovereigns in 1689. James fled to France.

Constitutional reform

Parliament passed a Bill of Rights barring any Roman Catholic from the **monarchy**, naming Mary's sister, Anne, as heir to the throne and insisting upon frequent Parliaments and free elections. At last, after six centuries, a degree of stability had been brought to the country and the powers of the king or queen strictly limited. In the Act of Settlement of 1701, the roles of Parliament and government were set out and

Catholic Ireland

When the Catholic English king James II was deposed in 1688, he went to Ireland and raised an army. However, in 1690, William of Orange defeated James's forces at the Battle of the Boyne. From then on, all Catholic Ireland was under English Protestant rule. In 1704, Catholics were forbidden to buy land, which excluded them from the Irish Parliament. In 1791, Societies of United Irishmen were formed in Irish cities and towns. They demanded that Catholics be restored their rights, the Parliament reformed and elections be introduced. A year later, the societies became a secret military organization. In **Ulster**, the northern area of Ireland, Protestants founded the Orange Order to protect themselves. Confrontations between Catholics and the **Orangemen** continue to this day.

their powers partially separated. In 1707, Scotland was incorporated officially into the United Kingdom. The Act of Union, as it was known, abolished commercial competition between the two countries and gave Scotland representation in the Westminster Parliament. Scotland was allowed to retain its own laws and its own church.

In 1714, the British **Crown** passed to the dukes of Hanover, who had been related to the British royal family. During this period, the power of the monarchy declined, and power passed to the king's first, or prime, minister, Robert Walpole (1676–1745), who was prime minister from 1721 to 1741. It is at this point that the history of Great Britain becomes that of its Parliament and ministers rather than the history of its monarchy.

After James II was deposed, many people – named 'Jacobites' – favoured his son, James Stuart. In 1715, James landed in Scotland, but his supporters were defeated in battle and he returned to France in exile.

Bonnie Prince Charlie

For a generation, relations between England and Scotland remained peaceful, and economic conditions in Scotland steadily improved. Then, in 1745, James Stuart's son, Charles Edward Stuart ('Bonnie Prince Charlie'), with French encouragement, raised a rebellion among the Highlanders of northern Scotland. He marched his followers as far south as Derby, but they were gradually driven back and finally defeated at the Battle of Culloden, near Inverness, in 1746.

The rebellion was suppressed with great brutality. **Jacobite** supporters were hunted down and either executed or transported to British colonies in the Caribbean.

This monument to the Jacobite Highlanders stands on the shore of Loch Sheil in Scotland. It was erected in 1815.

By 1700, the centre of the world economy had moved away from the Mediterranean to northern Europe. At this time, both London and Paris had populations of over half a million.

In the mid-18th century, the British empire was largely limited to North America, the Caribbean and trading posts on the Indian and African coasts.

Highlanders were prohibited from wearing their traditional tartan and from bearing arms, and the lands of leading Jacobites were seized. Charles was a fugitive for five months and eventually escaped to France.

THE GROWING BRITISH EMPIRE

Henry VIII had been the first monarch to establish an English navy. Under Elizabeth I, it was very much a freelance fighting force, but Charles I raised 'ship money' to make it the Royal Navy. By the beginning of the 18th century, the British navy was stronger than any other and claimed 'command of the seas'. It was the power of the Royal Navy that made it possible for the British to range ever further around the globe, seizing the colonies of other European countries and carrying troops to conquer new lands and establish new trading centres.

Colonization began on the North American mainland with the establishment of the colony of Virginia in 1607. The Pilgrim Fathers arrived in Massachusetts in 1620, and the colonies of New Hampshire, Rhode Island and Connecticut soon followed. By 1641, there were 20,000 English settlers in New England. New

THE BRITISH EMPIRE 1763

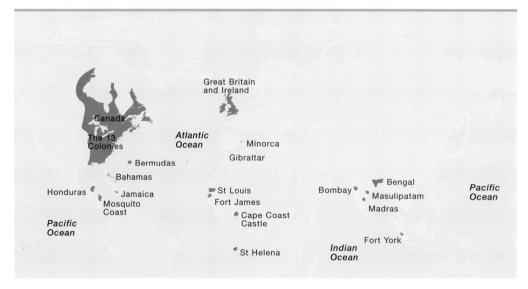

Netherlands was captured from the Dutch in 1664 and was renamed New York. Within little more than a century, there were thirteen flourishing colonies along the eastern seaboard, as far south as the Carolinas and Georgia. Off the coast, the Bermudas were seized in 1612.

Britain's major rivals in America were Spain and France. Spain's interest lay principally in South America, in the lands around the Caribbean and the Gulf of Mexico. The British were able to gain possession of the Bahamas, Barbados, Jamaica and some other smaller islands, but did not attempt the Spanish-held mainland. The French, however, claimed the whole of Canada, and were at war with Britain over its possession for nearly a century, until 1762.

It was not until the mid-18th century, with North American trade well established, that Great Britain began to look further afield. Trading in Africa proved difficult and was run from fortified trading posts. As early as 1600, the East India Company had been founded to trade with India and the East Indies (the islands of South-East Asia). However, it was not until the 1740s that the company came into direct conflict with the French and gained control of the east coast of India. Victory in the Battle of Plassey in 1757 made the East India Company masters in much of the Indian subcontinent. Finally, when Captain James Cook took formal possession of New Zealand and Australia for the British Crown in 1770, the foundations of the huge British empire, 'on which the sun never set', were laid.

At the beginning of the 18th century, Britain's position abroad was strong. Its colonial rivals – France, Spain and the Dutch Republic – had all been weakened by the War of the Spanish Succession, which ended in 1713.

In 1770, Captain James Cook charted the coasts of Australia and New Zealand, claiming both territories for the British Crown.

Loss of the American colonies

Jealous of Britain's increasing colonial interests in North America, France used assistance from the Native Americans to increase its attack on Britain's American colonies and threaten all-out war with Britain itself. The French trading posts on the west coast of Africa were captured, as was France's most important American fort at Duquesne on the Ohio River. In 1759, James Wolfe took Quebec for the British, and the French also suffered defeat in Europe. Peace was finally signed in 1763, and Britain became a world power for the first time in its history. This was achieved as much through trading overseas as by direct government intervention. The East India Company, a commerical concern that traded on the Indian subcontinent, had become so vast that it now employed its own army.

The Boston Tea Party

Meanwhile, trouble was brewing in the American colonies. The colonies had repeatedly asked for representation in the British Parliament with the slogan 'No taxation without representation'. Lord North, the prime minister, removed the duty on most English goods imported into America, but retained the tax on tea. When a shipment of tea was thrown into Boston Harbour in 1773, North suspended the **Constitution** of Massachusetts. This event became known as the Boston Tea Party. The subsequent battles between British troops and colonists at Lexington and Bunker Hill led to war. With the signing of the Declaration of Independence

> In the wars against France, Britain had a great military leader in John Churchill (later made Duke of Marlborough). Churchill was given money to build himself the only non-royal palace in the country, Blenheim. In 1874, it became the birthplace of 20th-century prime minister Winston Churchill.

Slavery

The British had been involved in the slave trade in Africa and the Caribbean for many years. Indeed, it was they who introduced the first slaves to Virginia in 1619, and slavery became common in many British colonies. However, as the 18th century progressed, a growing movement opposing slavery grew. This was led by the Quakers, who petitioned Parliament in 1783. In 1807, the British government banned the slave trade with the colonies and in 1834 banned slavery in the colonies themselves. In the British Caribbean colonies, a total of 776,000 slaves were freed.

in 1776 and the surrender of General John Burgoyne at Saratoga in 1777, it became very difficult for the British to continue the war. When the French gave assistance to the colonists in 1778, they were able to cut off the supply of troops by sea, and in 1781 the British army surrendered at Yorktown. The American Revolution had succeeded, and Britain had lost an important part of its empire.

The Napoleonic Wars and the Regency

The loss of the American colonies was followed by several years of political instability. Then William Pitt the Younger, who was only 24 years old, became prime minister in 1784. Great Britain was becoming increasingly wealthy thanks to the development of industry, and Pitt improved the country's finances by careful taxation.

The French Revolution of 1789, in which the French monarchy was overthrown, was at first welcomed in Great Britain, but the execution of the French king Louis XVI in 1793 provoked a negative reaction. Britain declared war against the French once more. Altogether, the war lasted 22 years. Napoleon Bonaparte became the French military leader and finally emperor of France. His armies won battle after battle on the European mainland, although the French fleet was much less successful against the British navy at sea. Horatio Nelson, Britain's most famous naval commander of the period, destroyed a French fleet at the Battle of the Nile in 1798, and in 1805 defeated a large fleet off Cape Trafalgar in Spain, although he was himself killed in the action. On land, Sir Arthur Wellesley (subsequently the Duke of Wellington) steadily drove the French out of Spain, and finally defeated Napoleon's army and put an end to his empire at the Battle of Waterloo in Belgium in 1815.

The insanity of King George III caused his son, the Prince of Wales, to be declared regent in 1811. He gave his title to the Regency style. Among the examples of the new style are Regent Street and Regent's Park in London.

The naval hero Horatio Nelson was killed at the Battle of Trafalgar, when a musket ball broke his spine.

The Industrial Revolution

The extensive coalfields that stretch from north-east England through the Midlands to south Wales, and the deposits of iron ore that conveniently lay alongside, were of great importance in the development of British industry during the 18th century. With James Watt's invention of the steam engine in 1781, coal suddenly became an important industrial fuel. It worked both ways: using coal-fired engines to drive pumps, it was possible to drain mines and dig deeper into the coal reserves. And the coal could be used to smelt iron ore, which would then be used to build the engines.

The introduction of machines resulted in a true revolution in everyday life. The textile industry was the first to be developed, even before steam-driven power was available. Agriculture, too, was affected. Jethro Tull invented a horse-drawn machine for planting seeds. The outcome was that many families became unemployed and were forced to leave the countryside for the towns to look for work. Spinning and weaving, which had been a **cottage industry**, were now concentrated in large mills, particularly in the county of Lancashire.

The population of England changed from being concentrated around London and the small market towns to the new industrial centres of the Midlands and northern England. Medical advances led to a dramatic drop in the death rate, and between 1760 and 1820, the population doubled from 7 million to 14 million.

The need to transport mass-produced goods – from the points of manufacture to their markets, both in Britain and abroad – led to rapid advances in canals (the Bridgewater Canal, 1765), railways (the Liverpool to Manchester line, 1830) and steamships (the *Great Western*, 1838).

THE VICTORIAN PERIOD

The Victorian period, the height of British economic supremacy, was named after Queen Victoria, the daughter of George III's fourth son. She was eighteen when she came to the throne and reigned for 64 years – the longest reign in English history.

The period is symbolized by the Great Exhibition of 1851 – a vast show put on in a specially built glass structure in London's Hyde Park to demonstrate to the world the strength of the British economy. It included products from all parts of the vast empire over which Victoria ruled.

Yet the Victorian period was also a period of great political and social change. The Reform Act of 1832, which had instilled the principle of popular representation, and the 1834 Poor Law began a move towards greater provision and representation for the poor. The products of this were the legalization of workers' associations and the rise of Chartism, a working-class movement demanding the vote for all men. This led to the Second Reform Bill of 1867, which extended the vote to most men. Successive governments introduced universal compulsory education and the legalization of trade unions. Between 1868 and 1881, William Gladstone and his political rival Benjamin Disraeli alternated as prime minister. These two men set the tone for much subsequent political debate in Great Britain. Horrified by the filth and poverty in which many British people lived, the German political writers Friedrich Engels (1820–95) and Karl Marx (1818–83) wrote the *Communist Manifesto* (1848).

The last years of Victoria's reign were overshadowed by the outbreak of war with Dutch settlers (Boers) in South Africa. The war began in 1899, and the Boers did not make peace until 1902.

The Crimean War

After 40 years of peace, in 1854 Britain – allied with France and Turkey – went to war with Russia. At the heart of the dispute was Russia's concern that Turkey controlled the straits giving access to the Mediterranean from the Black Sea. However, the quarrel arose over who should administer the Christian shrines in Jerusalem, which was then part of the Turkish empire. The war was fought principally in the Russian Black Sea peninsula of Crimea. It dragged on for three years, but after the fall of the fortress of Sebastopol, the Russians reluctantly made peace.

THE BRITISH EMPIRE 1820–1920

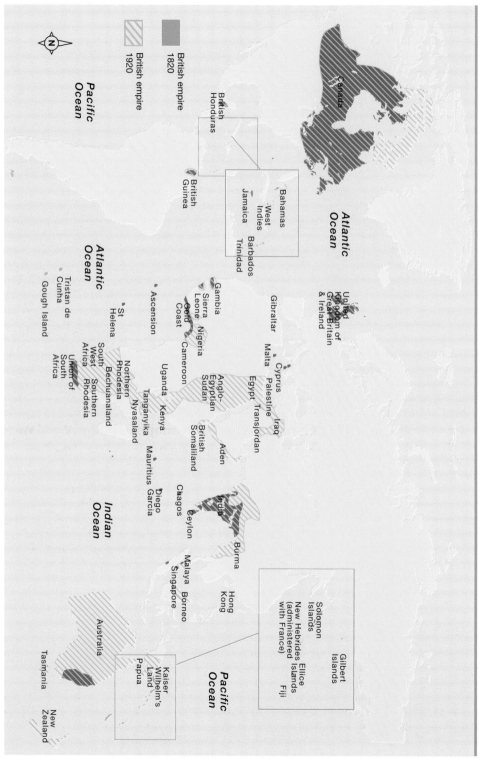

N

British empire
1820

British empire
1920

Pacific Ocean

Atlantic Ocean

Atlantic Ocean

Indian Ocean

Pacific Ocean

Canada

British Honduras

British Guinea

Bahamas
West Indies
Jamaica
Barbados
Trinidad

United Kingdom of Great Britain & Ireland

Tristan de Cunha
Gough Island

Gambia
Sierra Leone
Gold Coast
Nigeria
Cameroon

St Helena

Ascension

Gibraltar

Malta
Cyprus
Palestine
Egypt
Iraq
Transjordan

South West Africa
Union of South Africa

Bechuanaland
Northern Rhodesia
Southern Rhodesia

Uganda
Kenya
Tanganyika
Nyasaland

Anglo-Egyptian Sudan
British Somaliland

Aden

Mauritius
Diego Garcia
Chagos

India

Ceylon

Burma

Malaya
Singapore
Borneo

Hong Kong

Solomon Islands
New Hebrides (administered with France)
Ellice Islands
Fiji

Gilbert Islands

Kaiser Wilhelm's Land
Papua

Australia

Tasmania

New Zealand

Irish independence

When the potato crop failed in Ireland in 1848, as many as 1 million people starved to death. For others, emigration – mostly to the USA – was the only escape from the famine. In five years, the population fell by 2 million.

During the 1880s, there was a growing movement for **home rule** in Ireland, led by the radical Charles Parnell. Outbreaks of violence continued, until, in 1912, it looked as if a home rule bill would at last become law. However, the Protestant Ulster Unionist Party threatened armed resistance and began to import rifles. In 1913, the Catholic Irish Volunteers were formed in opposition and they also began to smuggle arms into the country. The secret Irish Republican Brotherhood raised a rebellion at Easter, 1916. After a week of street fighting in Dublin, the uprising was put down and its leaders executed by firing squad. The survivors formed themselves into the Irish Republican Army (**IRA**) and began a guerrilla campaign against the British administration. In 1921, after British attempts to contain the violence had failed, an Anglo-Irish treaty split Ireland into the independent Republic of Ireland in the south and the province of Northern Ireland in the north, the latter remaining part of the United Kingdom.

THE WORLD WARS

After unification in 1871, Germany became a major industrial and military power and began building a huge fleet of warships. This rivalled the maritime dominance of the United Kingdom's own navy, and in 1914, the UK and France went to war with Germany. What had at first seemed a relatively localized war became, with the entrance of the USA in 1917, a truly global conflict. When Germany surrendered in November 1918, more than 1 million young British men were dead.

The survivors, who had been promised 'a land fit for heroes to live in', found themselves in an era of financial instability and unemployment. The New York Stock Market crash of 1929 and the worldwide economic depression that followed resulted in more than 3 million people losing their jobs and surviving on the dole, a tiny welfare benefit. The British economy was saved by rapid growth in light engineering, such as electrical and

After World War One, the vote was extended to men over the age of 21 and women over the age of 30. This extension of the vote to many more working-class people led to the rise of the socialist Labour Party and the formation of the first Labour government in 1923.

The decline of manufacturing after World War One led to worker dissatisfaction and the General Strike of 1926 (above). The strike lasted nine days and involved half a million workers before being put down by the government and broken by the army.

machine parts, and the vehicle industry, which created jobs for many people and pulled the country out of recession. In Germany, however, Adolf Hitler's Nazi Party had come to power. Despite French and British attempts to curb the German leader's expansionist policies at Munich in 1938, the following year German tanks rolled into Poland. A treaty with Poland obliged the UK to declare war on Germany in September 1939.

Hitler's efficient fighting forces rapidly defeated Belgium, the Netherlands, Norway, Denmark and France. British forces were evacuated from France in May 1940. By June 1940, Britain was the only European country left to oppose Hitler. A ferocious German bombing campaign, known as the **Blitz**, rained down on Britain, destroying large parts of its cities. The pressure was relieved, however, when Hitler turned his attack on Russia in the summer of 1941. Following the Japanese attack on Pearl Harbour in December 1941, the USA also declared war on Germany. A huge **Allied** force landed in France in June 1944, and Germany surrendered in 1945.

At the end of World War Two, Britain found itself in a worse situation than in 1918. Bombing had destroyed heavy industrial plants, and the machinery that remained was old-fashioned and inefficient. In addition, important areas, such as the London and Liverpool docks, had been badly damaged. Financial aid was given to the countries of Europe in order to rebuild their shattered economies, and supplies were airlifted from the USA.

THE POSTWAR PERIOD

The efficiency of the wartime government, which required a national alliance of the main political parties and depended on strict planning of the economy, gave the British a taste for the planned programme of the **Labour Party** led by Clement Atlee (1883–1967). This plan involved the creation of the National Health Service, free universal education to the age of fourteen and the **nationalization** of the UK's major industries, such as vehicle manufacturing and steel production, and of the major utilities, such as water and energy production. In the last years of the 1940s, the country was still suffering the after-effects of the war, and shortages led to the rationing of food, clothing and other essential goods.

In April 1949, the UK, the USA, Canada, France and the Benelux countries signed the North Atlantic Treaty, which committed its members to mutual support against any threat of aggressive action by the former Soviet Union. From this treaty was formed the North Atlantic Treaty Organization – better known as NATO.

The Suez Crisis

One event that illustrated the decline in the UK's international status was the Suez Crisis of 1956. The Suez Canal in eastern Egypt runs from the Mediterranean Sea to the Red Sea, thus saving ships coming from Europe the need to travel around the coast of Africa in order to reach India and the Far East. In 1956, the canal was partly owned by the British and French governments, who had paid for its construction. When the Egyptian president Gamal Abdul Nasser attempted to take the canal into public ownership and to seize the large fees from ships in order to pay for a dam in southern Egypt, the French and British governments sent troops into the Suez area. However, at this point the two world powers of the period, the USA and the former Soviet Union, expressed their disapproval of the invasion, and both Britain and France were forced into a humiliating retreat.

New Elizabethans and the end of the empire

The 1960s in the UK were characterized by a more relaxed attitude, with British pop stars such as the Beatles, fashion designers such as Mary Quant and models such as Twiggy (below) becoming famous internationally. The capital became known as Swinging London, and young people rebelled against the authoritarian attitudes of their parents who still remembered the bleak postwar period.

Despite the creation of the **welfare state**, the Labour Party was defeated by the **Conservative Party** in the elections of 1951, and the Conservatives remained in power for the next thirteen years. The coronation of Elizabeth II in 1953 was used as an attempt to boost morale after the harsh conditions of the postwar years, and the population was encouraged to look forward to a new 'Elizabethan Age'. In fact, the country's position in the world had declined dramatically since before the war. Former colonies were given their independence, less from a sense of justice to the people who lived in these countries than from the simple fact that the UK could no longer afford to maintain its possessions overseas. India gained independence in 1947, Malaya in 1953 and Kenya in 1963.

The white heat of technology

The reconstruction of the UK's cities and **infrastructure** in the 1950s led to an economic boom, which continued into the 1960s. The prime minister Harold Macmillan (1894–1986) told the country 'You've never had it so good'. But taking advantage of the confusion in the Conservative Party after a government scandal, the Labour Party won the 1964 election. Harold Wilson (1916–95), the Labour leader, spoke of the 'white heat of technology' – new inventions that he claimed would boost the economy.

Crisis? What crisis?

Although in the 1960s the British economy appeared to be improving, a rise in world oil prices in 1973 brought a serious economic slowdown. The trade unions took advantage of the government's difficulties and demanded better wages for workers and introduced a three-day working week, effectively bringing the country to a standstill. The Conservative government of Edward Heath (born 1916), which had taken over in 1970, was forced to call a general election, asking 'Who governs Britain?'. The response was clear. The Conservative administration fell in 1974, but the Labour government that followed was seen as being unable to control union power. Prime minister James Callaghan (born 1912) returned from a holiday to find uncollected rubbish piled up on the streets of London. When asked about the crisis, he famously replied 'Crisis? What crisis?'. The period became known as the 'winter of discontent' and in 1979 ushered in the UK's first female prime minister, Margaret Thatcher (born 1925).

Margaret Thatcher

Born in 1925 the daughter of a Midlands grocer, Margaret Thatcher entered Parliament in 1959. Her rise to power was fast, and by 1970 she had joined the inner circle of the Cabinet in Edward Heath's Conservative government as Minister of Education. In 1975, however, she ran against Heath for the Conservative leadership and won a surprise victory, becoming the first woman leader of a major British party. Margaret Thatcher was, and remains, one of the most controversial figures in British politics. Her supporters claim that she saved the country from domination by the unions and revolutionized working practices in Britain. Her opponents credit her with destroying British manufacturing and opening divisions in British society that have never been healed. Perhaps her most famous quote was the statement that there was 'no such thing as society, only men, women and families'. Whatever Thatcher's enduring influence may be, she was unquestionably the major British political figure of the late 20th century. Many felt that her successor, John Major, suffered from her excessive influence.

Thatcherism

Thatcher's programme was to curb union power and to sell off state-owned industries to the private sector (individual investors) – hoping to create more competitive industry – and to end the unions' domination of political life. The effects of her policies were particularly dramatic in the north of England, where manufacturing was strongest. A worldwide recession in the early 1980s did nothing to ease the situation and, with industry stripped of government money, unemployment spiralled to over 3 million.

The 'troubles'

In 1939, the Irish Republican Army (IRA) began a terrorist bombing campaign in Belfast and several English cities. The IRA continued attacks against British military posts in Northern Ireland, increasing during the 1950s.

It was 1962 before the IRA formally called off its campaign.

During the 1960s, Roman Catholics began to protest against the Protestant domination of government in Northern Ireland. In 1968, these protests led to violent confrontations between Protestants and Catholics in Belfast and Londonderry. In 1969, the political division of the IRA, Sinn Fein, voted against any renewal of terrorism, but some of the delegates walked out of the meeting and created a 'provisional' Sinn Fein and a 'provisional' IRA to continue the attacks.

The IRA demanded the expulsion of British armed forces from Northern Ireland and the end of Protestant domination of public life. The campaign became one of Catholic against Protestant, often involving innocent civilians in Northern Ireland and England. In response to the IRA's campaign, Loyalist Protestant militia, which attacked Catholic targets, were formed. In 1972, the British government suspended the constitution and Parliament of Northern Ireland, and thereafter British troops became a permanent presence in the region. The worst years of violence were in the early 1970s, when several hundred people on each side were killed each year.

The inability to resolve the 'troubles' led the IRA to seek secret meetings with the British government in the early 1990s. It was hoped that the Good Friday agreement of 1998, organized by US senator George Mitchell, would bring peace. In early 1999, a new Northern Irish government was formed, including Protestants and members of Sinn Fein. In 2002, it was suspended for the fourth time since its beginning. The peace process is currently in a state of deadlock.

Thatcher rode out the storm, however, and when Argentina invaded the British-held Falkland Islands in the south Atlantic in 1981, the British 'task force' that was sent to recapture them and the resulting victory created a surge in support for the government. Thatcher was re-elected in 1983. The following year, a strike led by the mining union protesting at the closure of coal mines seemed about to challenge the government as miners had done in the early 1970s. The union lost its struggle, however, and over the next decade, the mining industry was effectively closed down.

Boom, bust and sleaze

Thatcher won her third election victory in 1987, and by 1988, was the longest-serving British prime minister of the 20th century. The introduction of a new community tax to pay for local services was hugely unpopular, however, and led to riots in central London. This, combined with what was seen as the prime minister's increasing arrogance, led to her losing the leadership of her party in November 1990. She resigned in favour of her chancellor (finance minister), John Major (born 1943). Despite Major's re-election in 1992, a series of economic failures and the public view of the Conservatives as corrupt led in 1997 to a landslide victory for Labour leader Tony Blair (born 1953), the first Labour prime minister to take office in eighteen years. Blair was re-elected in 2001.

POLITICS AND GOVERNMENT

The UK is a parliamentary **democracy**: the party that wins the most votes forms the government, and the government is directly responsible to Parliament. Parliament is divided into a lower house – the House of Commons – and an upper house – the House of Lords. All people over the age of eighteen are eligible to vote, but voting is not compulsory. Parliamentary, or general, elections are held every four or five years and can be called at any time by the prime minister. There are currently 659

In addition to the Parliament at Westminster, the British people also elect 70 members to a European Parliament based in Brussels, Belgium. Members of this Parliament represent constituencies (districts) throughout the European Union and pass legislation on social and economic mattters. In recent years, there has been a major debate in Britain about the increasing power of the European Parliament.

The prime minister has the right to go to the monarch at any time and ask for Parliament to be dissolved for a general election. Although governments can run up to five years, prime ministers often call an election early if they feel they have a better chance of winning.

The House of Lords

The House of Lords is the second chamber of the British Parliament, and it amends or rejects legislation of the House of Commons. The house is composed of hereditary **peers** or aristocrats – who traditionally passed down their right to sit in the chamber to their heirs – and life peers – members who were nominated by the main political parties and whose right to the title dies with them. Life peers are usually ex-politicians or major figures from public life. In addition, the chamber contains a number of bishops and senior judges. In 2000, the Labour administration abolished the right of hereditary peers to sit in the House of Lords. Ninety-two of them were allowed to keep their seats in the chamber until final reforms were made, in order to ensure that the legislative process was not interrupted. Further reforms to the chamber are proposed, and it is likely that in future the Lords will be at least partly elected.

constituencies (political districts) in the UK. Each constituency is roughly of the same size, representing between 50,000 and 80,000 voters. The king or queen is the head of state, but the present Queen acts entirely on the advice of the prime minister, the ministers and Parliament and has little or no say in political affairs.

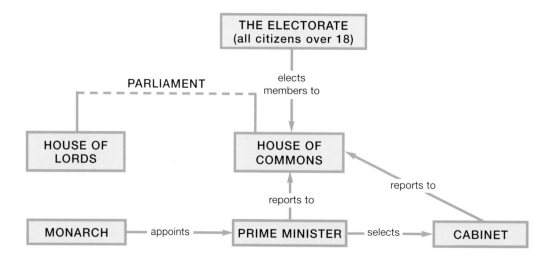

THE BRITISH PARLIAMENT IN 2002

Prime minister: Tony Blair

House of Commons
659 members • last election 2001 • elections held every five years or less

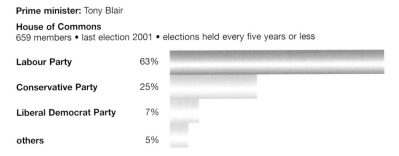

Labour Party	63%
Conservative Party	25%
Liberal Democrat Party	7%
others	5%

The government

Although the role of prime minister is similar to that of a president, the prime minister is not elected directly by the people but appointed by the monarch. However, in practice, the prime minister is always the head of the party that wins the most seats in a general election. The prime minister appoints the Cabinet, or council of senior ministers, which manages the government and its policies. Each minister is responsible for a different government department.

The Opposition is formed by the largest minority party. The main aims of the Opposition are to constructively criticize government policy and new laws, to seek amendments to, or to oppose, government proposals and to put forward its own policies. Members of the Opposition form a shadow Cabinet in Parliament, which mirrors that of the actual government.

Political parties

Since 1945, either the Conservative or the Labour Party has formed the government. Traditionally, the Conservatives favour free enterprise, while the Labour Party support more government intervention in the economy and welfare benefits for the poor and needy. The Liberal Democrats have remained very much a minor force, while two nationalist parties – Plaid Cymru (for Wales) and the Scottish Nationalists – have held only a few seats. There are several small Northern Irish parties.

British prime ministers since 1945:
- Clement Atlee (1945–51)
- Winston Churchill (1951–5)
- Anthony Eden (1955–7)
- Harold Macmillan (1957–63)
- Alec Douglas-Home (1963–4)
- Harold Wilson (1964–70)
- Edward Heath (1970–4)
- Harold Wilson (1974–6)
- James Callaghan (1976–9)
- Margaret Thatcher (1979–90)
- John Major (1990–7)
- Tony Blair (1997–)

The economy

*'If we command our wealth, we shall be rich and free;
if our wealth controls us, we are poor indeed.'*

18th-century British statesman Edmund Burke

The United Kingdom underwent fundamental changes in its economy in the last part of the 20th century. Service industries such as banking and insurance replaced the traditional manufacturing sectors of steel and vehicle production. Since the mid-1970s, the country has enjoyed the benefits of substantial oil and gas deposits extracted offshore in the North Sea. These have replaced coal mined in south Wales and northern England as the principal source of the country's energy supply. In the 1980s, many previously government-run industries, such as telecommunications and some vehicle manufacture, were privatized (sold off to private investors), and today, the government takes a much smaller role in industry than previously. At the beginning of the 21st century, the United Kingdom is a world leader in financial services, pharmaceuticals and defence industries, and has the fifth-largest economy in the world.

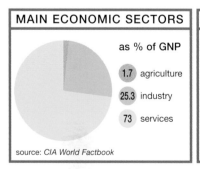

MAIN ECONOMIC SECTORS

as % of GNP

- **1.7** agriculture
- **25.3** industry
- **73** services

source: *CIA World Factbook*

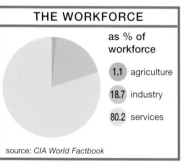

THE WORKFORCE

as % of workforce

- **1.1** agriculture
- **18.7** industry
- **80.2** services

source: *CIA World Factbook*

Richard Rogers's design for the insurers Lloyds' London headquarters, completed in 1984, marked the City's re-emergence as a world financial centre.

MAIN TRADING PARTNERS

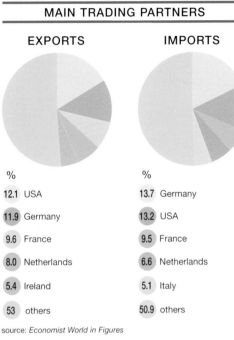

EXPORTS		IMPORTS	
%		%	
12.1	USA	13.7	Germany
11.9	Germany	13.2	USA
9.6	France	9.5	France
8.0	Netherlands	6.6	Netherlands
5.4	Ireland	5.1	Italy
53	others	50.9	others

source: *Economist World in Figures*

Although the UK shows a deficit in its trade balance, it has a surplus thanks to its financial services industry.

Since the 5th century, the UK's wealth was built on the wool from huge numbers of sheep, herded on the country's northern uplands. With the **Industrial Revolution** in the 18th century, coal, iron and steel, ships and railways, as well as finished cotton goods, brought the country continuing wealth. Industrialization also led to the construction of an efficient transportation system of railways, roads, canals and docks. As the manufacturing industry developed in the 19th century, the expanding British empire provided a ready market. The UK dominated world trade in the 19th century, but suffered setbacks in the mid-20th century.

MAJOR SECTORS

Today, manufacturing industries are still a major part of the British economy, although this proportion has declined sharply in recent years. Service industries, such as banking, insurance and tourism, now play a much more important role in the economy, employing 80 per cent of the workforce.

E X P O R T S

I M P O R T S

EXPORTS (£000 m)		IMPORTS (£000 m)	
manufactured goods	148.7	manufactured goods	156.8
food, beverages and tobacco	11.4	ood, beverages and tobacco	16.6
energy products	11.3	energy products	7.0
raw materials	2.8	raw materials	6.4
total (including others)	176.1	total (including others)	188.4

source: *Economist World in Figures*

Agriculture

Compared to other members of the **European Union** (EU), the UK employs far fewer people in agriculture, and the sector contributes less to the gross national product (GNP). However, British agriculture is remarkably efficient, producing 60

A place in Europe

The United Kingdom joined the European Economic Community (EEC) in 1973. The principal purpose of the EEC was to remove trade restrictions between the member nations. The EEC became the European Union (EU) in 1993, and the intention of the EU was to bind these nations even tighter into a single economic trading area. A single European currency, the **euro**, was introduced on 1 January 1999 in several EU countries, including three of the major European powers – France, Italy and Germany. The euro replaced the national currencies in 2002. So far, however, the UK has declined to introduce the euro. Supporters of the EU see it as a trading bloc that will eventually rival the economies of North America.

- European Union member countries
- non-member countries

per cent of the country's food needs with less than 2 per cent of the workforce. Farming was damaged in the 1990s by BSE (see right) and by fears over food safety. Agricultural productivity has risen in recent years thanks to improvements in farm machinery, seeds and plants, and the increased use of pesticides, herbicides and fertilizers.

About 74 per cent of the UK's land is dedicated to agricultural use, mostly for grazing or grassland. More than half of the farms are employed in livestock farming, such as cattle for dairy products and beef, and sheep for wool and meat.

Most crops are grown in eastern and southern England and in eastern Scotland. Chief among these are wheat, barley and rapeseed. Other crops include peas, beans and sugar beet. In recent years, there has been

The discovery of thousands of cases of BSE – a brain disorder that affects cattle – in British beef in the early 1990s devastated British farming. In 2001, foot-and-mouth disease threatened farming throughout Europe.

HOW THE UNITED KINGDOM USES ITS LAND

- crop land
- forest
- pasture
- mountains

Crop land in Britain is largely limited to the low-lying eastern region, while the country's westerly uplands are used for grazing sheep and cattle.

growing concern about the effect chemical fertilizers and pesticides have on humans and the environment. Organic farming methods – in which no artificial fertilizers or pesticides are used – are growing in popularity, and most large supermarkets in the UK now stock organic farm produce.

Forestry and fishing

Great Britain was once almost entirely covered with woodland and forest, but now only remnants of the great forests can be found. Today, about 10 per cent of land in the UK is forested. Much of this is commercial forest area with fast-growing conifers in Wales and north-eastern Scotland. The UK produces only about 15 per cent of the timber it needs, and the timber industry employs less than 1 per cent of the workforce.

The fishing industry comprises both deep-sea fishing and fish farming. The UK **imports** more fish and fish products than it **exports**, and the industry employs less than 1 per cent of the workforce. Concern about overfishing has led to restrictions on deep-sea fishing. In 2000, EU quotas on cod fishing in the waters of the UK were halved and money was provided to support the communities that depend on the fishing industry. It is still an important source of employment in coastal areas of Scotland and southwestern England.

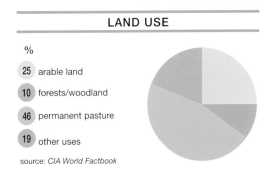

LAND USE

%
- 25 arable land
- 10 forests/woodland
- 46 permanent pasture
- 19 other uses

source: *CIA World Factbook*

An ancient stone circle stands before the cooling towers of Sellafield – the first full-scale nuclear power plant in the world – which opened in Cumbria in 1956.

Energy production

During the Industrial Revolution, great quantities of coal were required to fuel British factories. The vast coal reserves were often located near iron deposits, which greatly helped the iron-smelting and steel-manufacturing industries to develop. Coal mining became one of the UK's greatest sources of wealth. However, by the mid-20th century, the industry was in serious decline and many mines were closed, particularly during the 1980s.

The discovery of oil fields beneath the North Sea and the beginning of production in the mid-1970s proved to be a great boost to the country's finances. The UK now exports around half of all the oil it extracts.

Offshore gas fields were discovered in the 1960s, and today, the gas used in homes is natural gas, whereas previously it was manufactured from coal. Nuclear power provides about 26 per cent of the country's electricity needs. However, the safety of nuclear power plants continues to be a controversial subject in the UK.

ENERGY SOURCES

%

72.3 fossil fuels (coal, gas, oil)

26.4 nuclear power

1.3 hydroelectric power

source: *CIA World Fact Book*

The city of Aberdeen has enjoyed a boom in the last twenty years, based on revenues from the offshore oil industry.

In 1997, the British government abandoned the policy of linking aid with trade. This policy had tied provision of aid to poorer countries with contracts for British firms. Aid is now given to poorer countries without any specific economic ties to the UK.

Manufacturing industries

Despite the decline in manufacturing in the UK in the 20th century, it continues to be an important part of the economy. Just under 20 per cent of the workforce is employed in manufacturing, accounting for about 25 per cent of the GNP. After World War Two (1939–45), much of industry was **nationalized** – brought under government control – such as the railways, gas and electricity services, coal mines, steel manufacturing and shipbuilding. Under the four successive **Conservative** governments of 1979–97, many previously nationalized industries were sold to private investors (see box opposite). This was an attempt to expose industry to competition with foreign companies, thus ensuring that British companies kept up to date with the latest developments, while at the same time eliminating the need for government subsidies. Sometimes this has proved successful, as in the case of British Airways. However, in the case of the railways, passengers have seen ticket prices soar and a deterioration in services and safety.

In the 1970s and 1980s, British manufacturing industries, which had relied for more than a century on overseas sales, found it difficult to compete with other countries. This was partly because its industry was

Privatized industries

When the Conservative Party came to power in 1979, many important industries, such as water and energy companies, transportation companies – including airlines and railway lines – and even manufacturing – such as vehicle and steel producers – were owned by the government. In difficult economic circumstances, these companies received subsidies, while at other times, they provided the government with income. Some argued that subsidies made the companies, many of them monopolies (the only company providing a service), unresponsive and a drain on government resources. As a result, the government began to privatize, selling the companies to private investors.

By the time that Margaret Thatcher left office in December 1990, one in four of the United Kingdom's population owned stocks and more than 40 former state-owned industries had been **privatized**, affecting more than 600,000 workers.

Although some smaller companies were privatized in Margaret Thatcher's first term in office (1979–83), it was not until 1984 that the programme really got underway, with the privatization of the Jaguar car company and the sale of British Telecom (BT). The sales made large profits for small investors when share prices soared. The BT sell-off was followed by the privatization of British

Gas in 1986, and of Rolls-Royce, British Airways and the British Airports Authority in 1987 – the year of Thatcher's third election victory. British Steel (1988), the regional water companies (1989) and the electricity distribution companies (1990) were also sold off.

The Conservatives argued that the privatization programme left company directors free to act without interference from government and that revenues from

the sales were given back to the public in the form of tax cuts. Their detractors pointed to jobs lost in the state sector and argued that tax cuts benefited those on high incomes more than the poor. They likened the whole process of privatization to 'selling off the family silver'.

Privatization has influenced not only many foreign governments, from the Czech Republic to New Zealand, but is now also accepted by the leadership of the current **Labour** government in the UK.

MAJOR INDUSTRIES

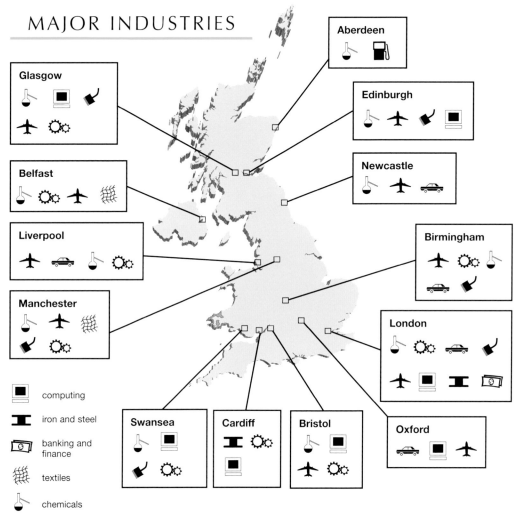

Aberdeen

Glasgow

Edinburgh

Belfast

Newcastle

Liverpool

Birmingham

Manchester

London

	computing
	iron and steel
	banking and finance
	textiles
	chemicals
	oil and gas
	electronics
	engineering
	vehicle manufacture
	aerospace

Swansea

Cardiff

Bristol

Oxford

Britain's industrial centres are still much the same as those of the mid-19th century.

undercut by the emerging economies of Asia, where wages were much lower than in the United Kingdom. A large part of what remains of heavy industry, vehicle manufacture and even service industries such as water supply have been taken over by foreign companies.

In the late 20th century, British manufacturing expanded into hi-tech industries such as computing, fibre optics and robots. Scotland is a major producer of computers, with about 40,000 people employed in the electronics industry in the so-called Silicon Glen – the area between Edinburgh and Glasgow. New computer industries are also located to the west of London in towns such as Reading and Windsor. There is a large research and **biotechnology** industry centred around the major universities of Oxford and Cambridge and around the cities of Manchester and Leeds.

Service industries

In 1997, the service industries, including finance, tourism and transportation, accounted for 73 per cent of the UK's GNP and employed 80 per cent of the workforce. Banking and finance have always been important to the UK's economy, and the City of London has long been one of the world's most important financial centres. London handles 20 per cent of the world's insurance and is the largest centre for foreign exchange.

Visitors to the UK come from all over the world, and the tourist industry plays a vital part in contributing to the country's income. Tourism accounts for more than 5 per cent of the GNP. In 1997, about 27 million people visited the UK from overseas. More visitors come from the USA than from any other single nation. Visitors are attracted not only by the country's natural beauty but also by its rich cultural heritage of historic houses and

MAIN FOREIGN ARRIVALS

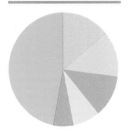

%

14 USA

13 France

12 Germany

8 Ireland

6 Netherlands

47 others

source: UK Government

The rise of the City

Although the City of London had long been a centre for international commerce and trading, it was with the Big Bang of 1986 that it secured its continuing position at the forefront of international finance. The Financial Services Act of 1986 and the Banking Act of 1987 deregulated financial services, merging the roles of dealer in stocks and shares and the broker who dealt directly with the public. Foreign banks were allowed to own brokers and themselves to join the London Stock Exchange. Deregulation created a mass of takeovers and share prices soared. This Big Bang was spurred on by the government's privatization programme (see page 89). The Big Bang also had a profound effect upon the nature of the City itself, leading to a host of new buildings with vast trading floors.

Today, London has the third-largest stock market in the world (after New York and Tokyo). Invisible earnings, which include foreign exchange dealings and returns on foreign investment, make up over half the UK's export earnings.

The birthplace of William Shakespeare, Stratford-upon-Avon in central England, is a magnet for tourists. Among the attractions is the cottage, shown here, of Anne Hathaway, the playwright's wife.

castles, monuments and museums and galleries and theatres. London is crowded with visitors throughout the year, especially during summer.

TRANSPORTATION

As a maritime nation, the UK has always been dependent on its ports for trade. Only recently, with the growth of air transportation and a decrease in the UK's export of heavy goods, has the importance of these ports declined. Seventy British ports are regarded as commercially significant, among them Portsmouth, Bristol, Liverpool, Glasgow, Dover and London. Freight traffic through British ports still totals some 545 million tonnes (536 million tons) per year. There are about 3200 kilometres (2000 miles) of navigable rivers and canals in the UK, of which about 620 kilometres (390 miles) are used commercially.

Air travel

The growth of air travel has resulted in a revolution in British transportation. There are now 143 licensed civil airfields in the UK, and an increasing number handle international traffic. In the London area alone, there are five airports, through which some 95 million passengers (international and domestic) pass each year. London's Heathrow handles more international passengers than any other airport in the world and is the fifth-busiest airport in the world (after Chicago, Atlanta, Dallas and Los Angeles) in terms of all passengers, domestic and international. British Airways, which is privately owned, is one of the world's leading airlines and has flights to almost 90 countries. Smaller airlines operate services within the UK and to cities on mainland Europe.

TRANSPORTATION

As a major industrialized nation, the United Kingdom has an excellent transportation system, although recent changes in the way that this is managed have led to some problems. The main cities are linked by an efficient motorway system and by a modern railway network. In addition to several international airports, the country also has a variety of ferry routes, linking Great Britain with Ireland, Scandinavia and the European mainland.

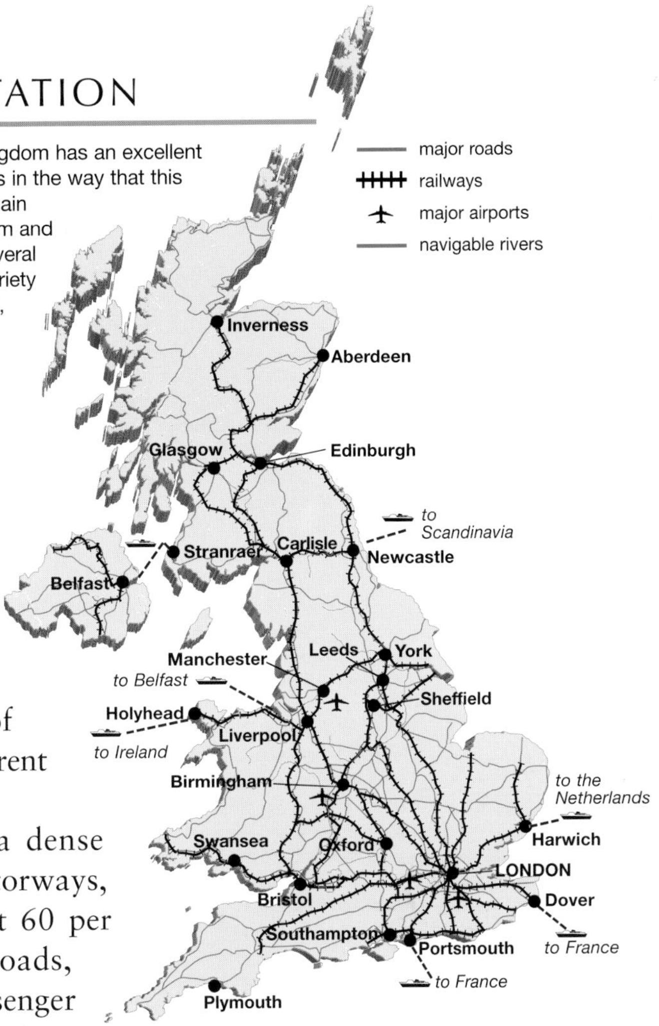

Map legend:
- —— major roads
- ┼┼┼┼ railways
- ✈ major airports
- —— navigable rivers

Map labels: Inverness, Aberdeen, Glasgow, Edinburgh, to Scandinavia, Stranraer, Carlisle, Newcastle, Belfast, Manchester, Leeds, York, to Belfast, Sheffield, Holyhead, Liverpool, to Ireland, Birmingham, to the Netherlands, Swansea, Oxford, Harwich, Bristol, LONDON, Dover, Southampton, Portsmouth, to France, to France, Plymouth

Rail and road

British railways were privatized in the early 1990s. Today, about 25 private companies run different parts of the country's railway system. This has meant that there is often a great difference in the quality of services that are provided in different parts of the country.

The United Kingdom has a dense network of main roads and motorways, particularly in England. About 60 per cent of freight is carried on roads, and about 90 per cent of passenger travel is by road, mostly by private car. Car ownership in the UK is high. About 70 per cent of British households own at least one car, although the figure is significantly lower than in France and Germany. In such a small country, the increasing use of the roads and motorways has led to enormous traffic congestion, especially in England and particularly in and around the major cities. Apart from concerns about the effects of pollution and sprawling road-building on the environment, roads are becoming a much less efficient way to travel. It is estimated, for example, that the average traffic speed in London is 17.5 kilometres per hour (11 miles per hour), which is slower than it was a hundred years ago.

Arts and living

'In England pop art and fine art stand resolutely back to back.'

20th-century English novelist Colin MacInnes

Unlike other countries in Europe, Great Britain developed little writing or art before the Roman occupation in the 1st century AD. It was not until the 7th and 8th centuries that outstanding written and illustrated works were produced.

Being an island, Great Britain developed separately from the European mainland so that, for example, the **Renaissance** came later to Great Britain, and then by way of trade and royal support. From the late 16th century on, however, Great Britain looked not to continental Europe but to territories further overseas. This expansion was reflected in changes in the English language, which, during the 16th and 17th centuries, adopted a multitude of terms from other languages. In the mid-18th century, Great Britain became the first **industrial** nation and moved away from the rural culture of country town towards the urban culture of the machine and greater social control. The Victorian period that followed still has an overwhelming influence on the structure of British daily life.

Today, the United Kingdom has a culture distinct from that of mainstream Europe. On one hand are the thriving music and art scenes and the media and fashion industries. On the other is a world of tradition that looks back to the country's illustrious past. British culture today is a blend of old and new, both of which make the UK the unique place it is.

Trooping the Colour, an annual pageant of marching bands to celebrate the Queen's birthday, is a typical display of British heritage.

FACT FILE

• Britain has the third-largest Internet industry in the world.

• The English writer Mary Ann Evans (1819–80) wrote under the name of George Eliot. Her novels, which include *Middlemarch* and *Daniel Deronda*, are now considered classics of English literature.

• Daily newspapers sell 332 copies per 1000 people in the United Kingdom, the eighth-highest rate in the world.

• The United Kingdom has the fourth-largest market for books in the world, with sales of £2875 million in the year 1997–8.

THE ARTS

The 600 years in Europe that followed the fall of the Roman empire (AD 476) have often been called the Dark Ages because so few works of art, or even writing of the time, have survived. Nevertheless, during this period Britain produced two outstanding works, the *Lindisfarne Gospels* (AD 698) and the *Book of Kells* (late 8th century).

Early artistic works

In most of Britain at that time, Christianity had a limited influence. However, in Ireland it spread during the 5th century AD, and in AD 563, an Irish monk named Columba (AD 521–97) established a monastery on the island of Iona, off Scotland's west coast. Soon afterwards, another monastery was built on the island of Lindisfarne in Northumbria. At this time, monks were one of the few groups that could read and write. At Lindisfarne they developed an intricate form of illustration, called illumination, which interwove the text of the Bible with coloured pictures and decorative Celtic patterns.

When the Vikings invaded Iona, many of the monks found refuge at the abbey of Kells in Ireland, and the *Book of Kells*, which had been started on Lindisfarne, was completed there. More complex in its decoration even than the *Lindisfarne Gospels*, the *Book of Kells* was described later as being so beautiful as to be 'rather the result of angelic than of human skill'.

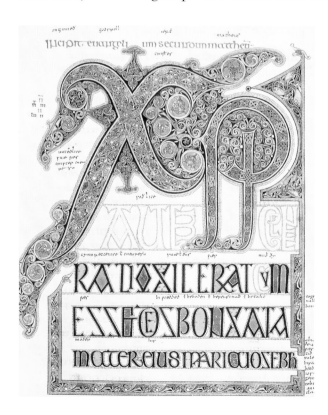

The opening page of the 'Book of Matthew' from the Lindisfarne Gospels *was completed at some point between 698 and 701. It is one of the masterpieces of medieval book illustration and is now kept in the British Library.*

Painting and sculpture

In decorative and pictorial art, Great Britain lagged behind mainland Europe for many centuries. The great Renaissance (rebirth) of painting and sculpture that began in Europe in the 14th century had no counterpart in Great Britain. In fact, as late as 1536, it was a German, Hans Holbein (1497–1543), who was appointed court painter to Henry VIII, and his were the only major works of art produced in England over a long period. While he was at Henry's court, Holbein also painted a number of miniature portraits, and these inspired the Englishman Nicholas Hilliard (1547–1619) to produce many exquisite miniatures during the reign of Elizabeth I.

William Hogarth (1697–1764), a Londoner, was one of the first English artists to paint and make engravings of ordinary people. Here, in a scene from his series A Rake's Progress *(1733), a man weds a wealthy widow for her money.*

King Charles I commissioned a number of great paintings from the Flemish painters Peter Paul Rubens (1577–1640) and Anthony Van Dyck (1599–1641), but it was not until well into the 18th century that a British school of painting began to emerge. Until this time, most of the successful artists in Great Britain had been foreign, and their work consisted almost entirely of portraits of rich people, with occasional pictures of scenes from classical myths.

The Royal Academy of Arts was founded in London in 1768. Its annual exhibitions of the work of members, and other selected artists, have continued to the present day. The first president of the Royal Academy was Joshua Reynolds (1723–92), who had studied painting in Italy. He installed himself as a portrait painter. Most of the 40 members of the academy had to make a living by portraiture, but some began to turn to landscape painting. Outstanding among these was Thomas Gainsborough (1727–88), who was born in Suffolk. Besides portraits, he also painted scenes of life in the countryside.

When he died in 1851, Turner left more than 300 paintings, nearly 20,000 watercolours and 19,000 drawings to the British nation. His The Fighting Temeraire *now hangs in the National Gallery.*

Landscape painting

Gainsborough's successor as a painter of the British landscape was John Constable (1776–1837). He based his style on the realism of Dutch painters and tried to capture the changeability of the British weather and seasons. His contemporary was Joseph Mallord Turner (1775–1851), who took landscape painting even further, flooding his canvases with shimmering light, through which the subject emerges hazily. Many of his paintings foreshadowed

the work of the later French Impressionist painters, and he is recognized as one of Britain's greatest painters.

Also a contemporary of Constable and Turner was the visionary poet and artist William Blake (1757–1827). His works were unlike anything that had been seen before. Many were hand-coloured engravings, and most were of religious or mythical subjects. Some people at the time thought he was mad, but his reputation has grown.

The work of the poet William Blake was based on his devout religious beliefs. He believed that an angel once came and visited him in his garden at Lambeth in south London.

After this flowering of British painting at the beginning of the 19th century, art in Great Britain went into decline. Technically, the paintings produced by British artists were excellent, but, with a few exceptions, their treatment was heavy and uninspiring. At the beginning of the 20th century, most British painters continued in the outdated style of the French Impressionists of an earlier generation.

It was the Surrealist exhibition of 1936 that opened the eyes of British artists to other ways of representation. Graham Sutherland (1903–80) was deeply affected by it and developed a very personal style, both in landscape and in portraiture. His former pupil, Francis Bacon (1909–92), began to produce highly dramatic figure paintings during the 1940s. Many, in thickly applied paint, sometimes smeared in places with balls of newspaper, are based on photographs or reproductions of famous paintings. Bacon is now recognized as an international master. Other British painters who have achieved worldwide recognition in recent years are David Hockney (born 1937), with his almost graphic style, using planes of bright colour, and Lucian Freud (born 1922), who paints realistic portraits with thick layers of oils.

Young British Artists

The director of a major advertising agency, Charles Saatchi, is responsible for the encouragement of the latest movement in art, known as Young British Artists (or YBAs). The most famous of these are Tracey Emin (born 1963), Sarah Lucas (born 1962) and Damien Hirst (born 1961). Hirst is renowned for exhibiting the preserved bodies of animals, cut into sections, in transparent cases filled with formaldehyde.

Until the 20th century, British artists showed little interest in sculpture. The work of Jacob Epstein (1880–1959), who moved to England in 1905, marked a turning point. Henry Moore (1898–1986) developed an individual figurative style and Barbara Hepworth (1903–75), an abstract style from the 1930s.

In 2000, the international collection of modern art of the Tate Gallery in London was moved to this renovated power station on London's South Bank. The gallery is called the Tate Modern.

Cathedral architecture

The architecture of the British Middle Ages (from about the 5th century AD to the mid-15th century) produced many remarkable monuments. With their soaring spires and vast interiors, England's Gothic cathedrals – which were built in the medieval market towns – are some of the country's architectural marvels. Outstanding among these is the beautiful cathedral at Salisbury in Wiltshire, which was mostly built between 1220 and 1258. It has 'as many windows as days in the year, as many pillars as hours and as many gates as moons'. The spire, which was not completed until the 14th century, is the tallest in England.

Not far to the west is the cathedral at Wells in Somerset (above), which was begun in 1185 and finished four centuries later. The western face of the building once carried 400 statues of kings, saints, apostles and angels. Some of these were destroyed in the 17th century by the **Puritans** (see page 63) but many remain.

Another great cathedral that was constantly added to over some 400 years is that of the city of Gloucester. Begun in 1089, it reveals the development of architectural styles over the centuries and has a magnificent stained-glass window behind the altar. In York the cathedral is known as the Minster and was built between 1220 and 1472. Its east window, the largest work of medieval stained glass in the world, was shattered during a fire in 1984. With great care and dedication, the 40,000 fragments have been reassembled.

British architecture

Apart from a few buildings that date from **Anglo-Saxon** times, some of the oldest buildings in the UK date from after the Norman Conquest of 1066. Most notable among these are the White Tower, which is part of the Tower of London (see page 53), and Durham Castle in the north of England. Norman architecture is characterized by huge, soaring arches and enormous columns. The period from the 12th to the 15th centuries saw the development of the Gothic style of architecture, used to splendid effect in the nation's cathedrals (see box opposite).

From the end of the 15th century until the early 17th century, architectural features from the Italian Renaissance, such as ornate decoration, began to appear in English buildings. In the 17th century, Inigo Jones (1573–1652), influenced by Italian architects, began to introduce some of their ideas into British architecture. Christopher Wren (1632–1723) was, in turn, influenced by Jones. After the Great Fire of London in 1666 (see page 64) had destroyed much of the city, Wren designed more than fifty churches in London, many of which still stand today, including the imposing St Paul's Cathedral.

The revival of Gothic architecture in the mid-19th century was an attempt to find a style of architecture that was genuinely English. It was felt at the time to be uniquely spiritual and therefore particularly suited to religious buildings.

The architecture of the Victorian era (1837–1901) borrowed from a variety of different styles, among them a revival of the earlier Gothic style. The Houses of Parliament in London were built during this period.

In the early 20th century, the Scottish architect Charles Rennie Mackintosh (1868–1928) developed a more modern style for British buildings. Mackintosh's style influenced later designers and architects.

Hi tech

Hi-tech architecture emerged in the UK in the late 20th century. Influenced by the design group Archigram in the late 1960s, two young British architects, Richard Rogers (born 1933) and Norman Foster (born 1935), developed a style using the properties of new materials and engineering techniques. Working with Italian Renzo Piano, Rogers designed Paris's Pompidou Centre (1971–7) and the Lloyds' Building in London (see page 82), while Foster has designed the Hong Kong and Shanghai Bank (1986) and the new Reichstag dome in Berlin (1999).

British literature

The Anglo-Saxons had a tradition of heroic poetry, often sung to the accompaniment of a harp, but few examples have survived. Some were eventually written down in the 10th century. The most famous of these is the 8th-century epic *Beowulf*, a story of the hero's struggle with monsters. After the Norman invasion (1066), Latin was generally used for prose writing, such as Geoffrey of Monmouth's *History of the Kings of England*, which was one of the earliest to relate the legend of King Arthur and his knights.

This stained-glass window from Canterbury Cathedral shows people travelling on a pilgrimage to the historic city. The stories of such pilgrims were used in Chaucer's The Canterbury Tales.

Early poetry of this period was often based on French sources and written in French, but gradually an English style developed. It flowered in the work of Geoffrey Chaucer (1342–1400), whose (unfinished) masterpiece is *The Canterbury Tales* (begun in 1387).

After Chaucer, writing in Britain tended to be of a serious, thoughtful nature. But during the late 16th century, a rich style of poetry and drama emerged, probably finding its finest expression in the work of William Shakespeare (1564–1616). Shakespeare developed a strong emotional style that has affected the work of writers ever since. Besides his 36 plays, he also wrote poems, notably a beautiful series of 152 sonnets (see opposite).

The two leading writers of the 17th century were both Puritans (see page 62). John Milton's (1608–74) *Paradise Lost* (1667) is a vast poem describing the fall of the rebellious angels from heaven and the expulsion of Adam and Eve from paradise. John Bunyan's (1628–88) *The Pilgrim's Progress* (1678) is a prose work portraying the journey of a pilgrim through all the troubles and temptations of the world to reach the Heavenly City. The work reflected Bunyan's personal religious experience.

The rise of the novel

The beginning of the 18th century saw British writers turning to novels – romantic fiction – that were meant largely to entertain. The first of these writers was Daniel Defoe (1660–1731), with adventures such as *Robinson Crusoe* (1719) and *Moll Flanders* (1722). A contemporary was the Irish clergyman Jonathan Swift (1667–1745). The first part of his satirical work *Gulliver's Travels* was published in 1726. These writers were followed by Henry Fielding (1707–54), whose finest work, which he described as 'a comic epic in prose', was the lengthy *Tom Jones* (1749). Another writer with a very personal style – he liked to begin by plunging straight into a conversation, often adding long digressions – was the parson Laurence Sterne (1713–68), who published his bestselling *Tristram Shandy* in instalments from 1760 to 1767.

Women writers

Very soon, women were joining the ranks of British writers. Ann Radcliffe (1764–1823) specialized in horror stories, such as *The Mysteries of Udolpho* (1794). Her example was followed by the young Mary Shelley (1797–1851) in 1818, with the horror story *Frankenstein*. In a very different vein, the gentle humour of English provincial life was brilliantly portrayed in the novels of Jane Austen (1775–1817), which include *Sense and Sensibility* (1811), *Pride and Prejudice* (1813) and her own satire on the Gothic novel, *Northanger Abbey* (1817).

Shakespeare's sonnet 18

Shall I compare thee to a summer's day?
Thou art more lovely and more temperate:
Rough winds do shake the darling buds
  of May,
And summer's lease hath all too short a date:
Sometime too hot the eye of heaven shines,
And often is his gold complexion dimmed,
And every fair from fair sometime declines,
By chance, or nature's changing course
  untrimmed:
But thy eternal Summer shall not fade,
Nor lose possession of that fair thou ow'st,
Nor shall death brag thou wander'st in his
  shade,
When in eternal lines to time thou grow'st:
So long as men can breathe or eyes can see,
So long lives this, and this gives life to thee.

The Gothic novel emerged in the 18th century and was characterized by startling events and gloomy horrors, which seemed to have a supernatural origin but were later discovered to have a rational explanation.

Scottish writers

In Scotland, creative writing was slow to develop. During the 18th century, much of the published work consisted of collections of traditional ballads (songs that tell a story) and airs. One of the principal contributors was the farmer Robert Burns (1759–96). He also wrote a large number of original poems, in both Scots dialect and 'correct' English, which became very popular. His birthday, 25 January, is still celebrated by Scots all over the world.

Another Scot who began by collecting traditional ballads was Walter Scott (1771–1832). He went on to write long romantic poems, and in 1813 turned his attention to the novel. Over the next fourteen years, he wrote 26 historical stories, which were all published anonymously, as well as a wealth of non-fiction. In 1827, he admitted to the authorship of the novels and added five more to his tally. The first of his novels was *Waverley* (1814), and the name 'Waverley Novels' has been given to the complete series.

Lewis Carroll's fantastical children's story Alice in Wonderland *(1865) was based on stories he had invented for a friend's daughter. Carroll was himself a distinguished mathematician who lectured at Oxford University.*

Charles Dickens

The leading novelist of the mid-19th century was undoubtedly Charles Dickens (1812–70). He began his career as a reporter of events in Parliament and also contributed articles to popular magazines. In 1836–7 he published *The Posthumous Papers of the Pickwick Club* in twenty monthly parts, which were an immediate success. Over the next 40 years, his output rivalled Scott's: seventeen novels, including *Oliver Twist* (1837–9), *David Copperfield* (1849–50) and *Great Expectations* (1860–1), as well as many other works and much journalism.

The 20th century

The early 20th century proved a particularly rich period for English literature. Novelists such as Virginia Woolf (1882–1941) in *To the Lighthouse* (1927) experimented with the form of the novel, while the US-born poet T. S. Eliot (1888–1965) used quotation and allusion in his *The Waste Land* (1922). Novelists Aldous Huxley (1894–1963) in his *Brave New World* (1932) and H. G. Wells (1866–1946) in his *War of the Worlds* (1898) and *The Shape of Things to Come* (1933) wrote of imaginary futuristic soci-

Irish writing

Ireland has a rich literary tradition for such a small population. The Irish-born playwright Oscar Wilde (1854–1900) enjoyed popular success with witty plays such as *The Importance of Being Earnest* (1895). Another Irish-born playwright with an international reputation was George Bernard Shaw (1856–1950), author of many plays on social themes. He won the Nobel Prize in 1925. James Joyce (1882–1941) was a more experimental writer. His greatest novel, *Ulysses* (1922), developed the technique known as 'stream of consciousness' – rather like a person speaking aloud his or her thoughts without any rational structure. Joyce's *Finnegan's Wake* (1939) is an almost unreadable experiment in the use of words. Joyce's disciple was Samuel Beckett (1906–89), an Irishman who wrote much of his work in French. He became famous following the performance in Paris in 1952 of his play *Waiting for Godot*.

eties. This tradition was given a distinctly political twist in the work of George Orwell (1903–50) whose *Animal Farm* (1946) and *1984* (1949) are modern classics.

After 1950, a number of British novelists became better known through film adaptations of their books. One of the first was Graham Greene (1904–91), who wrote the screenplay for *The Third Man* (1949). Among his novels that have been filmed are *Brighton Rock* (1938, filmed 1947) and *Our Man in Havana* (1958, filmed 1959). William Golding (1911–93) had an instant success with his first book, *Lord of the Flies* (1954, filmed 1963 and 1990). Golding received the Nobel Prize for Literature in 1983. Of recent authors, probably the most important are Martin Amis (born 1949) and Angela Carter (1940–92), the latter incorporating elements of fantasy and politics into her work.

The detective writer Agatha Christie (1890–1976) has sold over 100 million copies of her novels and has the distinction of the longest-running play in Britain, The Mousetrap, which has run continously in London since 1952.

British music

For several centuries, British music was very poorly regarded in other countries and largely neglected, even in Britain. Throughout the 18th century and much of the 19th, music remained a very minor art in Great Britain. Much of the credit for its revival must be given to the conductor Sir Henry Wood (1869–1944), who initiated the annual London Promenade Concerts in 1895 and used them as a showcase for developing British talent.

The first truly great composer to emerge in Great Britain was Edward Elgar (1857–1934). Elgar's orchestral work – such as the *Enigma Variations* (1899) and *Introduction and Allegro for Strings* (1905) – made his name well known, and he was knighted in 1904. Elgar's immediate successor was Ralph Vaughan Williams (1872–1958). His more familiar orchestral works – such as *Fantasia on a Theme by Thomas Tallis* (1910) and his nine symphonies – reflect the influence of both Elgar and the Finnish composer Jan Sibelius.

Benjamin Britten (1913–76) first made his name in 1945 with his opera *Peter Grimes*. Probably his most popular orchestral work is *The Young Person's Guide to the Orchestra* (1946), which takes a simple melodic theme that is played by each section of the orchestra in turn.

The German-born composer George Frederick Handel (1685–1759) moved to England after George I of Hanover became king. He directed opera in many London theatres and created many pieces of music for his royal patron, among them the *Water Music* of 1717. His most famous work is probably the oratorio *Messiah* (1742).

Henry Purcell

Purcell was born in London in 1659 and was trained as a choir singer before becoming Keeper of the King's Instruments in 1683. His work was limited because there was no public opera during his lifetime and he spent much of his time composing music for public theatres. Among his major works are the miniature opera *Dido and Aeneas* (1689) and incidental music for *A Midsummer Night's Dream* (*The Fairie Queen*, 1692). At his death in 1695, Purcell left over one hundred songs, many still played today.

Filmmaking

The leading director of the 1930s in the UK was Alfred Hitchcock (1899–1980), who began in silent films. From 1940, Hitchcock worked in Hollywood. Among his films, at least five are outstanding: *Spellbound* (1944), *Rear Window* (1954), *Vertigo* (1958), *North by Northwest* (1959) and *Psycho* (1960).

British rock music

The first British rock acts to achieve international success were the Beatles and the Rolling Stones. The Beatles (below, left to right, John Lennon, Paul McCartney, Ringo Starr and George Harrison) emerged from the Liverpool music scene of the early 1960s. Huge success in the UK soon led to vast record sales and 'Beatlemania' spread across the globe. In 1964, the Beatles held the top five positions in the US Billboard chart, the only act ever to achieve this feat. During the mid-1960s, they developed their own individual style in songs largely written by Lennon and McCartney. Perhaps their greatest work was *Sgt Pepper's Lonely Hearts Club Band* (1967), an album that used experimental recording techniques with traditional melodies. The Beatles continue to exert a huge influence on British music into the 21st century.

During this period, glam-rock performers such as David Bowie and Roxy Music were popular. In the mid-1970s, the Sex Pistols achieved notoriety with their version of punk rock. Since the 1980s, the music scene has been increasingly fragmented. Many young people go to clubs to enjoy different types of dance music, such as hip hop, garage, drum and bass and trance. Often the club DJs – who create distinctive and individual mixes from different record tracks – become more well known than the artists who make the music. Rock groups such as Oasis and Radiohead have achieved some level of international fame, but nothing approaching the hysteria of earlier decades.

Other British directors worked both in the UK and in Hollywood. Carol Reed (1906–76) received an Oscar nomination for his direction of *The Third Man* (1949), and finally the Oscar itself for the musical *Oliver!* (1968). David Lean (1908–91) won Oscars for *The Bridge on the River Kwai* (1957) and *Lawrence of Arabia* (1962).

In the 1970s and 1980s, two distinctly British forms of film emerged. The work of two directors, Mike Leigh (born 1943) and Ken Loach (born 1936), has achieved acclaim for its realistic depictions of working-class life. Notable are Loach's *Kes* (1969) and Leigh's *Life Is Sweet* (1990). In complete contrast was the 'heritage film', examples of which are the work of producer Ismail Merchant (born 1936) and the US-born director James Ivory (born 1928). Their dramas, such as *Howard's End* (1992) and *The Remains of the Day* (1993), achieved popular success, although they have been criticized for their idealized view of the British past.

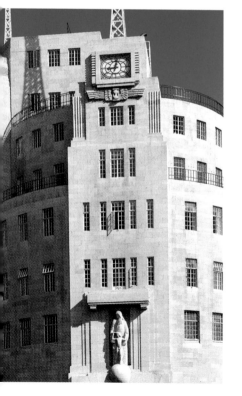

Broadcasting House, which sits at the top of London's Regent Street, is the centre of the BBC's radio broadcasts. Opened in 1931, the building is based on the shape of an old radio.

The media

For more than 30 years, broadcasting was a monopoly in the UK. The British Broadcasting Corporation (BBC) was first set up in 1922 and remained the radio 'voice of Britain' throughout World War Two (1939–45). In 1930, the BBC began television broadcasts, and in 1936 set up the world's first high-definition TV station at Alexandra Palace in north London. The BBC is not allowed to broadcast advertisements. It receives money from the government and from a licensing fee that everybody who owns a television set must pay. In 1954, the Independent Television Authority (ITA) was established to supervise commercial TV, and the first broadcasts carrying advertising began in September 1955. Independent television companies operate from some fifteen regional centres.

British newspapers

The ten principal daily (Monday to Saturday) and ten Sunday newspapers in the UK are distributed throughout the country. Nearly every household in the country purchases at least one of these. In addition, there are a number of daily and evening papers published in major regional centres – particularly Scotland – and many local weekly papers.

From 1785, *The Times* was the UK's leading daily newspaper, and for nearly two centuries was regarded throughout the world as the (unofficial) mouthpiece of the government. Since being bought by Rupert Murdoch's News Corporation in 1981, however, it has become a more standard commercial newspaper.

The Times, like its major competitors – the *Guardian*, the *Independent* and the *Telegraph* – is a broadsheet (a large-format paper). The independent *Financial Times* is internationally respected for its business news. Newspapers of a more popular nature, with larger readerships, are in tabloid form (approximately half the size of a broadsheet). The daily with the largest circulation is the tabloid the *Sun*, also owned by News Corporation, followed by the longer-established *Daily Mirror*.

Most daily newspapers also publish a Sunday edition, such as the *Sunday Times* and the *Observer* (the UK's oldest Sunday newspaper, founded in 1791 and now owned by the *Guardian*). The newspaper with the largest circulation of any in the Western world is the Sunday *News of the World*. It relies for its popularity on revealing the details of sordid scandals, especially those involving public figures.

Currently in Britain there are five land-based TV channels. Two are broadcast by the BBC (BBC 1 and BBC 2), and ITV, the principal commercial channel, carries the local regional station, together with contributions from other companies. Channel 4 provides a service that is less mainstream than ITV. Channel 5, which first broadcast in 1997, is the newest commercial channel. In addition to BBC local radio, there are numerous FM commercial radio stations. The BBC also maintains its World Service in radio and TV. This service, paid for by the British Foreign Office, broadcasts worldwide, and although it originated as a medium of the British empire, it has become an international news service with a worldwide reputation for journalistic excellence.

Channel 4 invests in modern British film and has had some notable successes, among them *Four Weddings and a Funeral* (1994) and *Trainspotting* (1996).

LIFE IN BRITAIN TODAY

Despite its reputation as 'the cradle of **democracy**', the United Kingdom remains a divided country in terms of wealth. The very rich get richer, while there are families who barely make enough money to feed and clothe their children. Although class distinctions have become blurred, the class structure still exists in the UK.

The British today enjoy free health care and a school education system that is free. The literacy rate is more than 99 per cent. Hobbies and sports are popular activities, and an estimated 29 million people participate in some kind of sport. The public house (or pub) is an important place for people, especially young people, to meet and talk. Although the UK is one of the most crowded countries in the world, many people say that they would not want to live anywhere else.

Food and drink

Despite its rather poor image overseas, British food can be, and often is, excellent. There is a rich tradition of farmhouse cooking, particularly in the north of England, and tasty cheeses such as crumbly white Lancashire, Wensleydale and Cheshire come from this area. The famous Cheddar cheese was originally made in the Cheddar region of Somerset, in the west of England. The industrial cities of the north are the home of the Lancashire hotpot, a dish made of mutton chops, onions and potatoes that was traditionally left to cook slowly all day until factory workers returned home. Yorkshire pudding is a tasty dish of cooked batter usually served with roast beef. The famous Melton Mowbray pork pie was created in the Midlands, but today the pork pie is a popular snack throughout the UK. Black pudding, a type of thick sausage made of cereals, pork fat, onions, sage and pig's

Enjoying a picnic at Royal Ascot races – one of the events attended largely by the upper classes. Others are the Henley rowing regatta and the Glyndebourne opera festival.

British beer and pubs

The British are known as a nation of beer drinkers. Until the 20th century, hundreds of breweries in England each produced their own characteristic beer. This was a 'live' beer, in which the yeast had not been killed by pasteurization, and the 'fizz' came from carbon dioxide naturally produced in fermentation.

Gradually, small breweries were bought up by large companies, who found it more convenient to pasteurize beer, pack it in aluminium kegs and pump in carbon dioxide. The quality of English beer fell rapidly, until a campaign was mounted by an organization called the Campaign for Real Ale (CAMRA). Now, many small breweries have been revived, some situated in individual pubs, each producing a distinctive brew.

In many of Britain's smaller towns and villages, the pub is the only social centre. Many provide food and rent rooms as well as selling beer and spirits. The design of the British pub is generally Victorian. Today, pubs built or refitted by large breweries are often decorated to look older than they really are and adopt deliberately unusual names.

---

blood, is traditionally a favourite in the north of England and the Midlands. It is usually fried and served for breakfast with bacon and eggs. Another fairly cheap and popular meal is the famous fish and chips. A portion of fish is coated with batter, which is then made cracklingly crisp by deep frying.

Scotland is famous for its porridge and haggis. Porridge is a breakfast dish made from oatmeal or rolled oats and flavoured with salt or sugar and served with milk. Haggis is made from sheep's heart, liver and lungs and oats. A sheep's stomach is cleaned and used as a skin to contain the mixture for cooking. Scotland's national drink, whisky, is world famous. Wales is the home of Welsh rarebit, a dish of melted cheese, sometimes mixed with beer, milk and flavourings, and spread on a slice of toast.

Cider is a sweet alcoholic drink produced from fermented apples and made in south-west England, particularly Somerset. Scrumpy is a more alcoholic version.

Cream tea

The cream tea is served in the south-west of England and is generally eaten in the afternoon. It consists of tea and scones eaten with jam and clotted cream (cream thickened by scalding). To make the scones you will need:

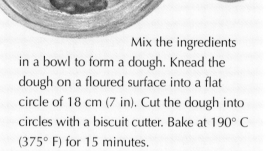

250 g (9 oz) plain flour
1 egg, beaten
2 teaspoons baking powder
85 g (3 oz) butter
85 g (3 oz) sugar
85 g (3 oz) mixed dried fruit
a pinch of salt

Mix the ingredients in a bowl to form a dough. Knead the dough on a floured surface into a flat circle of 18 cm (7 in). Cut the dough into circles with a biscuit cutter. Bake at 190° C (375° F) for 15 minutes.

The health of the nation

People in the UK enjoy a free health care system, called the National Health Service, set up in 1949. Everyone in the UK is entitled to free health care, regardless of their income. However, there are long waiting lists for non-urgent operations, and recently some people have chosen to pay for private health insurance. The UK also has an extensive social security system that provides unemployment and sickness benefits and cash benefits for families in need. Called the **welfare state**, it was established after World War Two (1939–45).

Education in the UK

Education is free and compulsory until the age of sixteen. Parents must pay fees for their children to attend **public schools** (which are usually boarding schools) and private schools. State schools are schools that are funded by the government. Ninety-three per cent of children are educated in state schools. Children in Scotland, England and Wales must go to school at the age of five, and at the age of four in Northern Ireland. Some children go to nursery school at the age of three or four.

England and Wales have a national curriculum of basic courses for students aged between five and sixteen, with tests at the ages of seven, eleven and fourteen to judge students' ability. The education systems in England, Wales and Northern Ireland are similar, but in Scotland the educational authorities are mostly independent from those in the rest of the UK. Some schools are affiliated to a religious denomination, such as **Roman Catholic** or Jewish schools. These, too, receive grants from the government to help with running costs.

Before leaving school at the age of sixteen, students take exams in various subjects, called GCSEs (general certificate of secondary education). Those who want to go to a university or on to further (vocational) education must study for another two years for advanced level examinations, called A levels. The proportion of people going into higher education has risen in the past ten years to about 50 per cent. A considerable number of new universities have been established since 1992, and former polytechnics – which concentrated on the sciences – have recently been upgraded to university status. There are more than 90 universities in the UK, including the famous Oxford and Cambridge universities that were established hundreds of years ago.

EDUCATIONAL ATTENDANCE	
college and university	50%
secondary school	97%
primary school	100%

Numbers attending university have risen steadily since the 1960s and are roughly the same as those of the UK's European neighbours.

The introduction of literacy tests at first proved controversial in British schools, but standards of work have risen as a result.

Ownership of long-lasting consumer products in the UK is comparable to that of the rest of Europe and the USA.

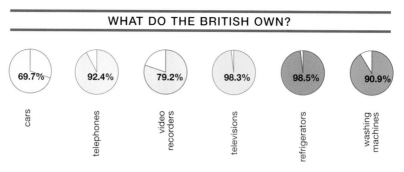

WHAT DO THE BRITISH OWN?

69.7% cars
92.4% telephones
79.2% video recorders
98.3% televisions
98.5% refrigerators
90.9% washing machines

source: *Encyclopedia Britannica*

Life in the home

The typical British home has hardly changed at all since the beginning of the 20th century. Most people still live in a house of five or six small rooms, made up of two or three bedrooms, a kitchen, living room and a bathroom.

Housing remains in short supply, and prices of homes in the cities and suburbs continue to rise. After 1945, people were rehoused away from city centres, often in the suburbs. As a result, city centres had little or no permanent residents. Very recently, however, the development of loft apartments – in empty warehouses, factories and even former hospitals and churches – has brought many people back to the city centres. Only those on higher incomes, however, can afford these apartments.

Religion

Until the break with the pope in the 16th century (see page 59), Britain was a Catholic nation. Since then, it has become overwhelmingly Protestant. Attempts were made to put down increasing Catholicism in the late 17th century and the mid-19th century, both instances resulting in an increase in the building of **Protestant** churches. There are a variety of non-conformist churches in the UK (those not associated with the established Church of England). These include the Baptists and Methodists, both of which were strong in Wales and in industrial areas in the 19th century. Britain's Jewish community, which had been expelled in 1290, received

HOW THE BRITISH SPEND THEIR MONEY

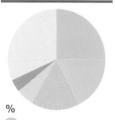

%
24.7 housing/energy
17.8 food and beverages
15.8 transportation and communications
5.8 clothing
4.1 health
6 recreation/culture
25.8 other

greater tolerance from the 17th century on and played an important part in 19th-century England. London's East End has traditionally had a large Jewish community. Today, although the Queen, who is the head of state, is also the head of the Church of England and bishops sit in the House of Lords, the UK is a largely secular (non-religious) country. Many people consider themselves non-practising members of the Church of England. Despite the role played by the Christian Church in the British state, the UK is a religiously tolerant society and there are large Sikh and Hindu communities from India and Kenya, Muslims from India, Pakistan, Turkey and the Balkans and a number of smaller religious communities.

> **The number of church attendees is higher among non-Christians than it is among Christians. Although 70 per cent of British people claim to be Christian, only 8 per cent of them regularly attend church.**

Sports and leisure

Games of all kinds have always been popular with the British, particularly the English. Indeed, it was largely the English who introduced many sports – such as lawn tennis, croquet, football, rugby and cricket – to the rest of the world. The game of golf, however, developed in Scotland.

Cricket is one game that still defeats most foreigners. For this reason, until very recently it was played only in England (not Wales or Scotland) and in certain countries of the former British empire, such as India. Its rules are so unusual that few people who have not grown up in one of the cricket-playing countries understand them. The typical cricket match – with its white-clad players on the village green, on club grounds or in a Test match between teams from different countries – appears to be a slow affair to the uninitiated.

England plays Scotland in the Six Nations rugby championship at the home of the English game at Twickenham in south-west London.

The future

'We are on a journey of renewal. Before us lies a path strewn with the challenges of change.'

British prime minister Tony Blair

It is difficult to predict the future of the United Kingdom. How far, in fact, will it remain 'united'? Two of the four national groups that make up the kingdom – Scotland and Wales – have already secured a degree of independence. And it is likely that eventually – although it may still take a generation or two – international pressures will result in Northern Ireland being reunited with the Irish Republic (Ireland). The contrast between the republic and Northern Ireland is dramatic, with the Irish Republic enjoying a new-found prosperity, while Northern Ireland has a high level of unemployment and remains a centre of unrest. However, a united Ireland could hope for further economic support from the **European Union** (EU), which would help boost the country's economy further.

On the other hand, neither Scotland nor Wales is presently capable of economic self-sufficiency, and London remains the financial driving force of the UK. For these countries to achieve independent status, the British government would have to make a huge financial investment in them. Such an investment would show no return for England and would leave England unacceptably weakened economically, most dramatically in its loss of North Sea oil and gas. Whatever the local ambitions in either country, Wales and Scotland are bound to remain within the UK.

The Eurostar terminal at London's Waterloo Station has trains that travel to the heart of Europe, a symbolic recent link with the continent.

FACT FILE

• The United Kingdom is the world's fourth-largest trader behind the USA, Japan and Germany and the world's third-largest trader including 'invisibles' (these include financial services and overseas investments) behind the USA and Japan.

• Since the early 1980s, when unemployment in the United Kingdom reached over 3 million, the figure has dropped below 1 million, and the government predicts a period of full employment in the near future.

• The UK is the world's sixth-largest energy producer.

A UNITED EUROPE?

At the same time, the nature of the United Kingdom's financial future is uncertain. The UK is a committed member of the EU, which is dedicated to the establishment of a single currency (the **euro**) and a centralized banking system. The European Monetary System (EMS) was designed to stabilize the value of the many currencies within the EU, allowing for variations of no more than 2 per cent in exchange rates. In 1992, the UK was obliged to withdraw from the EMS because it could not meet this requirement. When the euro was introduced as a common currency in 1999, the UK decided to delay adopting it. The UK's declared policy in 2002 was the intention to eventually accept the euro – but only 'when the time is right'.

The Bank of England in the City of London has traditionally controlled the money supply in the United Kingdom, but its influence may wane as that of Europe grows.

A political minefield

There is a lively political debate in the United Kingdom at present between those who seek closer ties with Europe and those who wish the country to remain more independent, relying instead on closer links with the USA. These two positions are roughly representative of the two main political parties, with the **Labour Party** favouring closer union with Europe, while the Eurosceptic **Conservative Party** seeks to keep the pound and a greater amount of political independence from the EU. There are members of both parties, however, who disagree with their own party's line, and the issue has become something of a political minefield for party leaders wishing to present a unified front.

The relationship between the United Kingdom and the USA continues to arouse suspicion in Europe, particularly in its leading members, France and

Germany. Indeed, the UK was originally prevented from joining the European Economic Community (the forerunner of the EU) because of this suspicion. For it to take its place and have its say in a united Europe, the UK must eventually become a fully integrated member of the EU. As the economic power of the EU increases, it may well be that the UK will then be forced to join completely with Europe and abandon hopes of closer trading links with the USA.

A service nation

The present financial stability of the UK – which can no longer rely on heavy industry for exports – is very dependent on the North Sea oil reserves and financial services. The UK is becoming a 'service nation', producing and managing services for other countries. This has always been part of the country's role, but the goods that are now moved around the world by British business are more likely to be financial investments, rather than manufactured goods.

Culturally, too, the United Kingdom has changed dramatically. During the second half of the 20th century, it gradually came to accept the fact that it was no longer a world power, reshaping itself instead as a modern European nation with a highly developed economy. The British accept today that they cannot impress their own culture on other nations. At the same time, however, strong historical links with a range of other countries greatly enrich the modern United Kingdom and make it one of the most culturally open and ethnically diverse nations in the world.

Ageing Brits

The United Kingdom has the thirteenth-oldest population in the world, with nearly 21% of people over the age of 65 in 2000. As in many other countries in western Europe, this presents economic problems for the government because shortly there will not be enough people working to provide tax revenues to pay the large state pensions bill. As a result, the government has taken steps to encourage young workers to immigrate from abroad and to ease immigration controls.

Almanac

POLITICAL

country name:
long form: United Kingdom of Great
    Britain and Northern Ireland
short form: United Kingdom

nationality:
    noun: Briton, the British (plural)
    adjective: British

official language: English

capital city: London

type of government: constitutional
    monarchy

suffrage (voting rights): eighteen years
    and over (not obligatory)

national anthem:
    'God Save the Queen'

national holiday: second Saturday of
    June (Queen's Birthday)

flag:

GEOGRAPHICAL

location: northern Europe;
    latitudes 50° to 61° north and
    longitudes 8° west to 2° east

climate: temperate, warmed by
    the Gulf Stream

total area: 244,820 sq km
    (94,500 sq miles)
    land: 99%
    water: 1%

coastline: 12,429 km (7723 miles)

terrain: hills and mountains in west
    and north, rolling plains in
    south and east

highest point: Ben Nevis,
    1343 m (4406 ft)

lowest point: the Fens, 4 m (13 ft)
    below sea level

natural resources: coal, oil, natural,
    gas, tin, limestone, iron ore,
    salt, clay, chalk, gypsum,
    lead, silica

land use:
    arable land: 25%

forests and woodland: 10%

permanent pastures: 46%

other: 19%

POPULATION

population: 59 million

population density: 241 people per sq km (624 per sq mile)

population growth rate (2002 est.): 0.21%

birth rate (2002 est.): 11.3 births per 1000 of the population

death rate (2002 est.): 10.3 deaths per 1000 of the population

sex ratio (2002 est.): 97 males per 100 females

total fertility rate (2002 est.): 1.7 children born per woman in the population

infant mortality rate (2002 est.): 5.4 deaths per 1000 live births

life expectancy at birth (2002 est.): total population: 77.9 years male: 75.3 years female: 80.8 years

literacy: total population: 99%

ECONOMY

currency: British pound (£); £1 = 100 pence (p)

exchange rate (2002): £1 = 1.6 euro(€)

gross national product (2000): £901,125 million (fourth-largest economy in the world)

average annual growth rate (1990–9): 2.5%

GNP per capita (2000): £15,244

average annual inflation rate (1990–2000): 3%

unemployment rate (2001 est.): 5.1%

exports (2001): £179,375 million
imports (2001): £210,625 million

foreign aid given (2000): £2813 million

Human Development Index
(an index scaled from 0 to 100 combining statistics indicating adult literacy, years of schooling, life expectancy and income levels):

91.8

TIMELINE—UNITED KINGDOM

World history

British history

50,000 BC

*c.***40,000** Modern humans – *Homo sapiens sapiens* – emerge

*c.***10,000 BC** First settlers on British mainland

3000 BC

*c.***1100 BC** Phoenicians develop the first alphabetic script

*c.***563 BC** Birth of Siddharta Gautama, the Buddha

*c.***3000 BC** Agriculture and pottery-making introduced to Britain

500 BC Iron-working introduced to Britain

100 BC

54–55 BC Julius Caesar makes raids on Britain

43 BC Romans conquer Britain

*c.***AD 1** Birth of Christ in the Roman province of Judea

AD 300 Scots make raids on Roman Britain

*c.***AD 380** Romans withdraw from Britain

AD 476 Goths sack Rome

1259 Hanseatic League formed by merchants in Germany

1206 Delhi Sultanate set up in India

1200 The Incas build the city of Cuzco in Peru

1096 First Crusade to reclaim Jerusalem begins

AD 1000

*c.***1000** Vikings reach American continent but do not settle

*c.***570** Birth of Muhammad at Mecca

AD 400

1381 Peasants' Revolt

1349 Black Death kills one-third of population

1337 Hundred Years' War begins with France

1305 William Wallace executed

1284 Treaty of Rhuddlan unifies England and Wales

1215 Magna Carta signed at Runnymede

1066 Norman Conquest

973 Edgar crowned first king of England

865 Danes land in East Anglia

793 Vikings raid monastery of Lindisfarne

597 St Augustine introduces Christianity

AD 577 Defeat of Celtic Britons near Bath marks rise of Anglo-Saxons

_c._1350

1453 Constantinople falls to the Turks

1492 Columbus lands in America

1520 The pope excommunicates Martin Luther from the Roman Catholic Church

1620 Pilgrim Fathers land in New England, USA

1485 Reign of Henry VII ends Wars of the Roses

1536 Dissolution of the monasteries and break with church in Rome

1588 Spanish Armada

1603 Accession of James I unites Scottish and English thrones

1649 Execution of Charles I leads to republican government

1660 Monarchy re-established under Charles II

2000 The West celebrates the Millennium – 2000 years since the birth of Christ

1989 Fall of communism in Eastern Europe

1979 Former Soviet Union invades Afghanistan

1973 World oil crisis

1969 First man lands on the Moon

2002 The Queen's Golden Jubilee

1997 Tony Blair's 'New Labour' wins landslide election victory

1982 Falklands War

1979 Margaret Thatcher becomes first female prime minister

1974 Miners' strike brings down Heath government

1967 Death penalty abolished

1945–51 Labour government introduces welfare state

1950

1750

1789 French Revolution begins

1799 Napoleon becomes emperor of France

1815 Napoleon defeated at Waterloo

1848 Famine prompts unrest in much of Europe

_c._1750 Industrial Revolution begins in England

1832 Parliamentary Reform Act

1851 Great Exhibition in London

_c._1870 USA overtakes Britain as largest world economy

1945 End of World War Two, defeat of Germany

1941–5 Holocaust of European Jews

1939–45 World War Two

1914–18 World War One

1940–1 The Blitz

1936 Abdication of Edward VIII destabilizes monarchy

1926 General Strike

1904 Entente Cordiale, treaty between France and Britain

Glossary

abdicate formally give up the throne

Allies Britain, France, Russia, the USA and other countries that fought together against the Triple Alliance in World War One and the Axis powers of Germany, Italy and Japan in World War Two

Anglo-Saxon Germanic people who settled in the island of Great Britain in the 5th century

barons aristocratic military commanders who controlled much of Britain during the Middle Ages

Benelux Belgium, the Netherlands and Luxembourg

biotechnology exploitation of biology, such as genetic engineering, usually for commercial purposes

Blitz large-scale bombing of London during the period 1940–1 (from the German *Blitzkrieg*, 'lightning war')

capitalism economic system based on supply and demand, and private ownership of businesses and industry

Celts ancient west European people with a complex culture, remnants of which remain in western Britain

Conservative Party main right-wing political party in the UK

constitution written collection of a country's laws, its citizens' rights and beliefs

cottage industry any small-scale industry or craftwork involving few workers

Crown institution of the monarchy; the king or queen

democracy country where the people choose their government by election, and where they hold supreme power

export product that is sold to another country

euro new European currency

European Union (EU) organization made up of European countries that work together on many economic, social and political issues

Gaelic Celtic language spoken in Scotland and Ireland

Gulf Stream warm ocean current that comes up from the Equator, bringing mild weather to the British Isles

henge prehistoric circle of vast stones or pillars of wood

Home Counties English counties that surround Greater London

home rule rule of Ireland by the Irish

import product that is bought from another country

industrial economy based on developed industries and infrastructure rather than on agriculture

Industrial Revolution explosion of new industrial techniques in northern England from about 1750

infrastructure basic framework of public works, such as transportation, building and public services

IRA Irish Republican Army – a terrorist organization that has fought for the union of the Republic of Ireland and Northern Ireland

Jacobite Catholic supporters of James Stuart and his descendants, who during the 18th century tried to overturn the Protestant monarchy

knight (verb) to make someone a knight (*Sir*), a public, non-hereditary and largely ceremonial title

Labour Party main left-wing political party in the UK

monarchy state ruled by a king or queen, or the institution of the royal family itself

moorland area of open, uncultivated land

nationalization taking of businesses or utilities into government ownership

Orangemen Protestant group in Northern Ireland

peer aristocrat; also previously a member of the House of Lords

privatization selling off of government-owned industries or concerns to the private sector

Protestant member of the branch of Christianity that developed from the Reformation and the ideas of Martin Luther

public school private fee-paying school

Puritans 17th-century Protestant group concerned with strict morals and modesty in public life

Regency period from 1811 to 1820, when the son of George III (later George IV) ruled in place of his father

Renaissance great revival of the arts and learning in Europe during the 14th to 16th centuries

Roman Catholic member of the branch of Christianity based in Rome whose spiritual leader is the pope

Royalist supporter of the royal faction in the English Civil War

Ulster ancient name for the area now covered by modern Northern Ireland

welfare state system whereby the government protects the health and well-being of those in need

Bibliography

Major sources used for this book

Davies, Norman, *The Isles* (Oxford University Press, 2000)

MacLean, Fitzroy, *Scotland: A Concise History* (Thames and Hudson, 1993)

Porter, Roy, *The Creation of the Modern World: The British Enlightenment* (Norton, 2000)

The Economist, *Pocket World in Figures* (Profile Books, 2000)

General further reading

Bennett, Lynda A. (ed.), *Encyclopedia of World Cultures* (G.K. Hall & Co., 1992)

World Reference Atlas (Dorling Kindersley, 2000)

The Kingfisher History Encyclopedia (Kingfisher, 1999)

Student Atlas (Dorling Kindersley, 1998)

The World Book Encyclopedia (Scott Fetzer Company, 1999)

Further reading about the UK

Lacey, Robert, and Danny Danziger, *The Year 1000: What Life Was Like at the Turn of the Millennium* (Back Bay Books, 2000)

Lenman, Bruce, *A History of Scotland* (Viking, 1992)

Paxman, Jeremy, *The English: A Portrait of a People* (Overlook Press, 2000)

Schama, Simon, *A History of Britain: At the Edge of the World 3500 BC–AD 1603* (Talk Miramax Books, 2000)

Some websites about the UK

British Broadcasting Corporation (BBC) *www.bbc.co.uk*

National Gallery *www.nationalgallery.org.uk*

Tate Gallery *www.tate.org.uk*

Index

Acknowledgements

Cover photo credits
Corbis: Catherine Karnow

Photo credits
AKG London: 56, 60, 63, British Library 96, Justus Gopel 48, Erich Lessing 97, 98, Schutze/Rodemann 100; **Corbis:** Roger Antrobus 17, Archivio Iconografico, SA 102, Dave Bartruff 111, Betteman Archive 76, 104, 107, Jonathan Blair 53, Chris Bland/ Eye Ubiquitous 42, Michael Busselle 28, Richard Cummins 14, Abbie Enock 23, Robert Estall 46, Macduff Everton/Mandm. Inc., Franz-Marc Frei 51, Gianni Dagli Orti 70, Philip Gould 88, George Hall 89, Brian Harching/Eye Ubiquitous 33, Dallas and John Heaton 41, John Heseltine 12, Angelo Homack 24, 108, 118, Jeremy Horner 30, 116, Martin Jones 26, John Michael Kielty 37, Christian Liewig/Temp Sport 115, George McCarthy 31, Chris Parker/ Cordaiy Photo Library 92, David Paterson 18, Stephan Rafferty/Eye Ubiquitous 78, Jim Richardson 65, Charles Rotkin 19, Sandy Stockwell/London Aerial Photo Library 35, Paul Thompson/Eye Ubiquitous 39, Patrick Ward 110, Julia Waterlow/ Eye Ubiquitous 38, Nik Wheeler 82, Jenny Woodcock/Reflections Photo Library, Adam Woolfitt 6, 32, 94, Michael S. Yamashita 44; **Hutchison:** Robert Francis 1; **PA Photos:** Yuri Mok 99; **Peter Newark's Pictures:** 59, 67, 69; **Robert Hunt Library:** 74